STREAMLINED
SEWING FOR FUN

STREAMLINED
SEWING FOR FUN

RENEE ROBINSON, *Des*.R.C.A. and

JULIAN ROBINSON, *Des*.R.C.A.

ST. MARTIN'S PRESS
NEW YORK

To

Charlotte, Xavier and Georgina

AFFILIATED PUBLISHERS:
Macmillan & Company, Limited, London
also at Bombay, Calcutta, Madras and Melbourne
The Macmillan Company of Canada, Limited, Toronto.

Contents

Acknowledgments

The authors gratefully achnowledge the generous
assistance given by the following in the prepara-
tion of this volume: J. & P. Coats Ltd., Sewing
Group;   Barney Blackley;   Lalage Waldman;
V. E. Robinson;   Kate Nash;   Mary Gilliatt;
Hornsey College of Art.

The Idea of this Book

The idea of this book—as with our two previous books, *Streamlined Dressmaking* and *Streamlined Curtains and Covers*—is to show how your sewing can be quick and easy to do as well as being thoroughly enjoyable and fun. It is based on completely new, streamlined methods which have been specially chosen for their simplicity and easy adaptability. Whether you would like to make cushions or soft toys, dresses or a garden hammock, the methods illustrated in this book will encourage even the most bashful to try—and to achieve instant sewing success.

The emphasis is on ease and enjoyment, and we have therefore avoided all the usual mumbo-jumbo of complicated and old-fashioned methods. To see just how easy sewing can be, we believe it is best to start by taking the plunge and making something: hence the first chapter showing simple ways of making soft toys. These are not only fun to make but provide sufficient sewing experience for even a beginner to tackle curtains, cushions, bedspreads or even a simple dress as an exciting challenge to be enjoyed.

Remember never let your sewing become dull or boring. Always be on the look-out for new ideas to make, as this is what makes sewing exciting. Magazines and newspapers provide a fund of ideas on decorative schemes, interesting surface treatments, novel ways of brightening-up dull things and the latest trends in design, so whenever you see something you like, make a note of it in a scrap-book, adding fabric cuttings, press photographs and articles, so that when you are thinking of making something new you can thumb through it to help crystallize your thoughts. A scrap-book kept up-to-date in this way will become as important to your sewing as your scissors or pins.

R. and J. R.

1. Making Some Simple Toys

In this chapter we shall explain many simple ways of making a variety of soft toys. The methods used are slightly unorthodox, and much frowned on by the traditional sewing schools, but they are easily understood and achieve quick results. Beginners should start by tackling some of the simplest felt animals, glove puppets or rag dolls before attempting the more complex Jack-in-the-Box or Doll's Basket. The excitement of a child receiving a boldly decorated Bunny Pop-Up will be much more rewarding than the disappointment aroused by an unfinished Hobby Horse.

The variations in soft-toy designs are infinite, but we have tried to cover most of the basic principles in this and later chapters as many more toys can easily be designed and made using the same general principles. Always be on the look-out for new ideas, for novelty is of great importance, and remember to note in your scrapbook any ideas you see in newspapers and magazines, on television programmes or in your local toyshop.

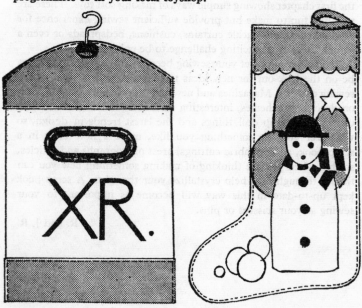

Toy post-box. Cut two oblongs of heavy scarlet cotton or sail cloth, 18″ × 36″, curving the top to fit the shape of a simple wooden coat hanger. On to the top of one piece stitch a piece of black felt 6″ deep, and on to the bottom a piece 4″ deep. Two inches below top piece of felt mark out and cut an oval letter-box hole 6″ × 2″, and bind the raw edge with matching bias binding. Lay the front to the back, right sides inside, and stitch along all edges, allowing a ½″ seam. Turn to right side through letter opening, and roll out and press edges. Now slip a wooden coat hanger inside centre top of curve, so that the hook goes through the stitching, and hand sew firmly into position. Stick on or stitch ribbon initials or other decorations, as required. A 12″ zip set into the bottom seam makes the recovery of 'posted' toys much easier, but is not essential. Whilst the smaller **Christmas Stockings** can be easily made from bold stocking-shaped pieces of coloured felt stitched together and decorated with stuck-on pieces of ribbon, coloured cut-outs and beads etc. **Toy mobile.** A variety of animals, fish, and other small toys made with brightly-coloured felts, stuffed with pieces of old stockings, and sewn or glued together at the edges, make most amusing toy mobiles. Suspend each one on a different

9

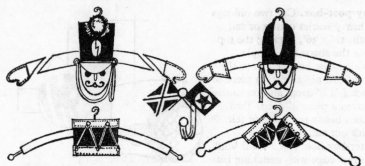

length of thick sewing cotton or twine fastened to a strip of thin wood about 8″ to 12″ long and ¼″ thick—plant stakes are ideal. As the weight of each mobile will vary with size, only a rough guide for setting them up can be illustrated. Simply experiment with different positions for your threads until evenly balanced.

Coat hangers. As the above illustrations show, gay and colourful coat hangers and coat hooks for the nursery can be made by simply decorating plain ones with pieces of brightly-coloured felt or fabric. Stick these into position with UHU glue, adding any other

novelties you choose, such as pieces of ribbon, beads or embroidery patterns, before finally securing with a few hand stitches for strength.

Pencil toys. Simple decorative pencil ends can be made in much the same way as described for coat hangers. In fact the few designs illustrated are all interchangeable; thus the design for a clown hanger could be used to make a clown pencil, and the design for a pig-topped pencil could be used to make a pig-topped coat hook. The important thing to remember is to cut good, clear shapes of coloured felt, sticking and

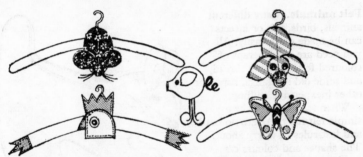

stitching on beads, ribbons and other novelty trimmings to give the effect required, before you finally secure into position with a few extra hand stitches.
Finger puppets. Finger puppets like those shown below are great fun, particularly for younger children. They are usually made around fingers of a disused knitted glove, or pieces of circular French knitting made through a cotton reel. However, they can be made by simply sticking a 2″ wide strip of felt into a cylinder and decorating in one of the ways shown below, or in any way you choose. Novelty is very important for finger puppets, as it is for pencil toys or nursery coat hangers, so simply experiment with beads, ribbons, embroidery stitches, or anything you think will make it look bright and gay or unusual.
Egg cosies. These are really like large finger puppets, and should be designed and made in much the same way, from the traditional chicken cosy shown on page 9—which is made out of yellow and red felt stuck and stitched together—to a moon rocket. Really, anything that works, that is fun to make, and which amuses the children, is a good egg cosy.

Felt animals. Many different animals, birds, fish or insects can be made quite easily. All you need are a few scraps of coloured felt, stitching thread, and some old stockings, kapok or other inexpensive stuffing.

When starting to make a simple felt toy there are no hard and fast rules to worry about. The shapes and colours can be chosen according to your own whim; if it looks amusing to you, and your children like it, then it is a good toy. Whereas a beautifully stitched one that nobody likes and the children won't play with is, undoubtedly, a complete failure.

In general, the basic method for making each toy is exactly the same, whether it is a cat, pig, duck or snail. Your first step should be to buy or make a simple paper pattern, the easiest of these consisting of just two body pieces. Cut out your felt to the shape of the pattern, and stitch the two pieces together $\frac{1}{8}''$ from the edge, leaving a $1\frac{1}{2}''$ opening along the tummy line for stuffing. Do this with pieces of stocking or kapok, then sew up the opening. You can then complete your animal by adding beads or buttons for eyes, embroidery stitches for a mouth, rug wool for a tail, etc.

Slightly more complicated animals require patterns similar to the one shown opposite, which consists of a main body

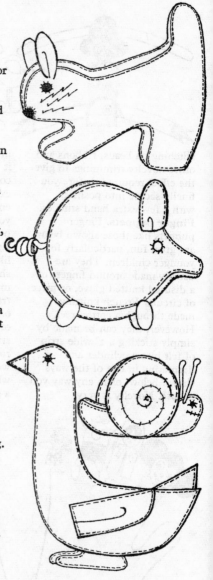

piece, under-body gusset, wings, tail and feet. Use the pattern to mark out the pieces of felt accurately, so that when they are stitched together at the edges each piece will fit neatly on to the next. Remember to leave a $1\frac{1}{2}''$ opening for stuffing. Finally, after the opening has been neatly stab-stitched together, add the eyes, beak and other features made much larger. Alternatively they could be made inside out, just like a normal cushion, with a $3''$ opening for turning through. However, do avoid using any small trimmings which are easily detachable, as these could be a potential danger to very young children. Generally speaking it is better to concentrate on large, bold

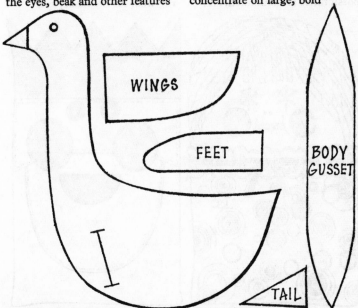

which can be made from a variety of materials, such as raffia, rug wool, beads, sequins, buttons, string and ribbons. **Animal cushions.** These can be made by following the same design and sewing instructions we have given for felt animals, only the cushions should be areas in striking colour combinations, rather than intricately sewn details. Another possibility is, instead of filling the animal with stuffing, to leave an $8''$ gap in the tummy and sew in a zip fastener, so that it can be used as a nightie case as explained on pages 15, 25 and 26.

Toy cushions are generally made out of two pieces of material cut to a rectangular shape, and simply turned through as explained on page 78. The success of the actual design and method of decorating them depends as much on the inventiveness of the maker as on her sewing skill. The design possibilities are unlimited, and

the right sides together and machine the edges ½″ in, leaving a 3″ opening at one end. Turn the cushion through this gap, and stuff with kapok or other inexpensive filling before slip-stitching gap together. Using UHU glue, stick on and stitch sections of coloured felt for the face, looped or knotted rug wool for the mane, and

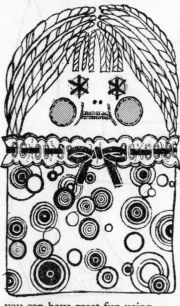

you can have great fun using your own ideas, or copying those you have seen in magazines, books, newspapers, or shop windows.

One of the simplest nursery cushions to make is the lion design, shown opposite. This is made from two pieces of 14″ × 9″ sand-coloured corduroy. Lay

plaited rug wool for the tail. Various sorts of embroidery stitches can be added for eyes, nose, mouth etc.

Another cushion based on the same shape, but this time made in printed and plain cotton fabric, is the doll-shaped cushion shown on the left, which has been decorated with lace, coloured felt, rug wool and ribbons. The King cushion is made in much the same way, only this time various pieces of coloured felt have been stitched on to the basic rectangular shaped background material.

Finally, the cow-shaped cushion is simply a normal 10″ square cushion made in cream-coloured woollen fabric, with

successfully by first roughing out the shape on a sheet of brown paper, in much the same way as described for simple dolls on page 22. As you can see, the possibilities are endless, and the scope for your own ideas is enormous.

Nightie cases. As explained on page 13, it is very simple to

contrasting patches of soft leather or felt, hand-stitched on, a stuffed and embroidered fabric and felt head, stuffed fabric legs, and a rug-wool tassel for the tail.

A lot of interesting and unusually shaped designs—such as a pig, snail, or owl-shaped cushion—can be made quite

turn an animal cushion into a child's nightie case. Simply make a gap in the tummy line of 8″ instead of 3″, and omit the stuffing. Sew in a bold zip along the tummy opening, and decorate the case in the usual way, adding felt cut-outs, rug wool, etc. For other ideas turn to page 25 and 26.

Glove puppets. On a piece of fairly stiff brown paper, measure out and mark a rectangle 6″ wide by 8″ deep, extending the top two corners upwards and outwards to form rough arm shapes. Take two oddments of printed cotton fabric, and cut them to the shape of your pattern. Place the pieces face to face and machine round the edges, allowing ½″ for the seam, and leave the bottom 6″ width open for the hand. To neaten this bottom part, simply turn under ½″ and machine.

Cut two oval shapes of plain cotton fabric, 2″ × 3″, to form the head. Stitch these together, leaving a 1″ gap for turning through and for stuffing with small pieces of stocking or kapok. Sew gap edges together, and hand-stitch head to centre of glove between the arm shapes. Finish head with sixpenny-sized felt eyes, stuck on and then stitched, embroidered nose and mouth, and rug wool hair. Decorate the body with lace and a jagged-edged felt collar, brightly coloured buttons and brass bells.

Pop-ups. These are made in a similar way to the glove puppets but are usually slightly smaller, approximately 4″ × 6″.

First make a tube or cone, 10″ × 6″, from a flexible piece of cardboard; or simply cut a ½″ hole out of the bottom of an empty food container. Cover the cone or tin with stuck-on patterned wrapping paper, tucking it over and in at the top and securely sticking this down with UHU or similar glue.

Draw out a simple puppet shape on a piece of paper, extending your top line to form the shape of two arms, and a head $2'' \times 3''$. Make as for glove puppet but adding felt bunny ears and a different face, as illustrated on the left. Now cut a piece of cane $14''$ long and insert it up through your puppet so that it goes $2''$ up into the head. Sew tightly round the neck to hold in position. Finally, push the stick down through the covered cone or tin, and stick the bottom edge of the puppet to the top edge of the cone.

Hobby horse. If you haven't a large, brightly coloured sock to spare, simply cut two pieces of patterned fabric to this shape, place them face to face and sew up the edges, leaving the top of the sock open. Turn through to right side, and stuff the foot section very tightly with pieces of stocking or kapok to form the head. Push in a brightly painted broom handle and stuff the 'neck'. Turn the opening in $1''$ and with several strands of button thread stitch it together, using very tight stitches around the broom handle, and adding extra stuffing as required. The handle can be even more firmly secured with two metal

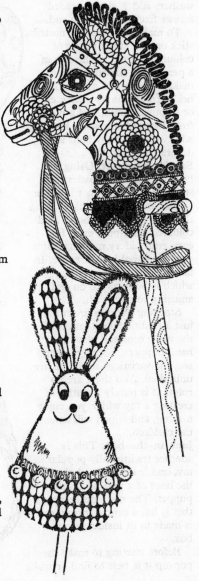

washers and $\frac{3}{4}''$ dome-headed screws fixed $1''$ from the end.

To make the eyes and nostrils, stick on and stitch pieces of coloured felt cut to the size of a penny and sixpence. Then make the ears and mouth. Make bridle from chunky piping cord or colourful braid, and a mane from loops of rug wool. Finally, add two brass baby bells and decorative studs.

Stocking puppet. Using a brightly striped or patterned stocking, form the foot into the face of an animal or insect along the lines described above. Add coloured pom-pom eyes, felt ears, embroidery markings, and even rug-wool hair or mane. In fact you can add anything which is both fun to do and amusing to play with.

Stocking puppets are really just a traditional extension of the more common glove or hand puppets, but as you can see, the variations in design are unlimited. And there are no rules. It is purely a matter of creating a toy which you enjoy making, and which will amuse the children.

Jack-in-the-box. This is another traditionally popular toy, and is constructed along the lines of a pop-up or glove puppet. The main difference is that is has a centre spring, and is made to fit inside a simple box.

Before starting to make the pop-up it is best to find or make

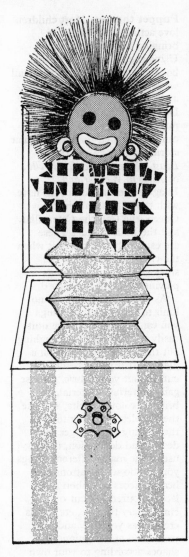

a straight-forward box, about 6″ square, with a hinged lid. Alternatively a food tin will do if you can fix on a cardboard lid which opens and closes on the hinge principle. Next, decorate the box with coloured wrapping paper, both inside and out.

Buy a suitable wire spring, or use the springs from three or four hair rollers joined together with twine or soft wire. To form the body, make a long thin tube cut out of coloured fabric, adjusting the size and shape to fit inside the box. Make a head out of a small foam-rubber ball, on to which you have fixed suitable markings for the features.

Sew the spring firmly to the inside of the body fabric, both top and bottom, adding a frill or bow at the neck to hide the stitches. Stick bottom firmly to inside base of box, and stab-stitch through box base to permanently secure.

If a food tin is used the fabric body section could be made 4″ shorter and fixed inside the top of the tin, as described for a Pop-up on page 16. The spring need not be fixed to the base of the tin but can hang freely, and of course there is no need to decorate inside. The outside, however, should be gaily decorated with stuck-on wrapping paper, or nicely painted, with added felt cut-outs and other novelties as required.

Jumping Jacks or doll puppets can be made out of pieces of brightly-coloured or patterned cotton and jersey fabric, rug wool, scraps of felt, pieces of ribbon and lace, odd beads, decorative buttons, embroidery cottons and oddments of braid, etc., and assembled in much the same way as the other toys already described in this chapter. The only difference is that you will need 1 yard of round black elastic, and 6″ of wooden dowelling ¾″ thick.

First make a simple doll or felt animal, as explained on pages 12, 23 or 29, adding the features, clothes and any other decorations you choose. Teddy Bright-Eyes—shown on the right—is based on a 10″ × 8″ glove puppet but with the arm and head sections made separately. These sections have been stuffed with pieces of stocking and then hand-sewn to the main body, which is made out of striped night-shirting.

Cut the round elastic into three equal lengths, and tie a firm knot at the end of each piece. Sew one piece, by the knotted end, to the back of each hand, and the third to the back of the head. The other end of the elastic is then attached to the wooden dowelling, either through holes made 1″ from each end, with one in the centre, or simply notched round the wood in these positions.

Puppet theatre. Most children love acting, and delight in bringing their toys to 'life'. Using the illustrations in this book as a guide you can make all sorts of 'characters' to act out a simple fairy story or play. Doll and animal puppets, glove puppets and stocking puppets can be designed for such popular stories as *Beauty and the Beast, Snow White, Cinderella,* or *Alice in Wonderland.* Imagine the fun you could have with the White Rabbit, the Queen, the Cat, the Caterpillar, and the Mad Hatter! These are especially fun to enact when the children can follow the story and music on a long-playing gramophone record.

As you can see, there is no limit to the variety of things you can design and make quite easily. Always start by roughing out the shapes you want on a piece of stiff paper before cutting out your fabric. Choose gaily patterned material, or brightly coloured felts, and use the simplest stitching to sew them. Ring the changes in design and decoration, making use of the many different things you can do with buttons and beads, pieces of ribbon and lace, coloured felt cut-outs, embroidery threads, etc. Be as creative as you like, and try your hand at designing new shapes according to your own ideas. Remember, there are no hard and fast rules to worry

about. If they please you, and your children like playing with them, then your toys are obviously successful. On the other hand a toy made strictly in accordance with the traditional sewing methods, which is beautifully sewn but not nearly such fun to make, or receive, is obviously a flop.

illustrated below. Add an extra $\frac{1}{2}''$ all round your pattern, but as it is best to make the head separately trace this on to another piece of paper before cutting straight across the neck.

Using your paper pattern as a template cut out two body sections in printed, striped, or brightly-coloured cotton fabric,

Simple dolls. Many simple doll shapes can be made by slightly adapting the methods already explained for animal and doll cushions, shown on pages 13 and 14. First of all you need to draw a paper pattern. Using a piece of stiff paper, rough out the pattern required by making a rectangle, $9'' \times 12''$, and shaping this along the lines

and lay these together, right sides inside. Stitch along the $\frac{1}{2}''$ allowance line, leaving the neck edge open. Next, cut two pieces of plain cotton for the head and stitch these together in the same way, allowing $\frac{1}{2}''$ for the seam and leaving the neck edge open.

Turn both body and head sections through neck gaps and

22

stuff with inexpensive filling. Sew head section to the main body by stitching at the neck.

Using rug wool for the hair, coin-sized pieces of coloured felt for the main features, and various simple embroidery stitches, decorate the face and head as required. Finish off the body stuffing from coming out or the decoration from coming adrift.

Basically they are made in exactly the same way as the simple dolls explained opposite, but they can also be made as small versions of the animal cushions shown on pages

section with oddments of lace, ribbon, decorative buttons, beads, pom-poms, etc., as shown on this page or elsewhere in the book, or simply according to your fancy.

Bean-bag toys. These are particularly fun for young children, provided the fabric cover and stitching are strong enough to prevent the bean 13 and 14. The only real difference is that dried beans, instead of kapok, should be used for the stuffing of the main body section.

Bean-bag toys may be decorated in much the same way as we have suggested for some of the other toys in this chapter, but as they are intended for very young children any

Sewing doll. First of all make a simple doll in the way we have already described, but fill the main sections with dried beans instead of kapok. On to this main shape stitch several large felt pockets, or layers of flat aprons or petticoats, so that the pockets can be used to hold scissors, tape measures, reels of cotton, etc., whilst the felt apron, or tie, can be used for pins and needles.

Pencil case. Any one of the dozen or so simple dolls already illustrated could be made into an attractive pencil case, simply

trimmings which are easily detachable are a potential danger and should be avoided. It is better to concentrate on large bold areas of strong fabric, using striking colour combinations, rather than intricately sewn details.

Useful dolls. These are dolls which can be used as pencil holders, needle cases, comb or hairbrush holders, etc. All you need to do is follow the methods explained on pages 22 and 23 for making a simple doll, and then adding such embellishments as wide pockets, a gay felt apron, wide belt, or sew in a zip with a large bold ring for easy opening and closing.

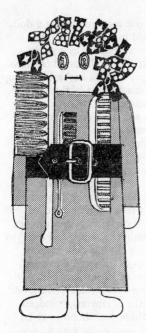

a large pocket this can be used for such things as hair slides or ribbons. Decorate the face and head with an 'early-morning look', by using hair curlers and ribbon bows instead of hair.

Decorative cases. There are many other decorative cases which are also easy to design and make apart from the four shown here and illustrated on the next two pages, including nightie cases, hot-water bottle covers, travelling nappy cases, or cases for many similar purposes. The basic methods for making each one are the same, with only the size and decoration being varied as desired.

1. Cut a rough paper pattern to

by omitting the stuffing and leaving a large enough opening in one of the side seams to insert a zip, which should be firmly stitched into place. Alternatively a slit 8″ deep can be made down the centre front and a bold ring-ended zip surface-stitched over this in a similar way to that shown on the right.

Morning tidy. Make a simple rectangular bean-bag doll as already explained. Around the middle tie a simple webbing belt, stitching this firmly into place each side. Into the belt slot a comb, brush, tooth-brush, etc., and if you have given your doll

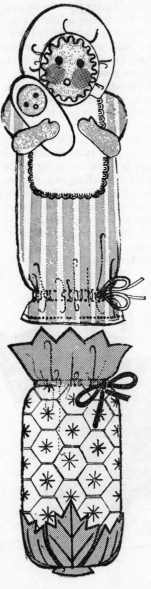

the size required, using a doll, folded nightie or a child's hot-water bottle as a guide. Next add 1″ all round the basic shape, without bothering to copy the exact shape of the stopper or other intricate detail, as for this you need only draw a smooth curve.

2. For an average-sized hot-water bottle cover, or decorative nightie case of similar size, the material required would be $\frac{1}{4}$–$\frac{1}{2}$ yard of terry towelling, needlecord, velvet curtaining, corduroy or something similar, and an 8″ to 10″ zip. In addition several pieces of coloured felt, small pieces of lace or crochet, coloured embroidery silks, odd lengths of ribbon, or indeed anything you choose, can be used for the decoration.

3. Cut two identical pieces of fabric to the size and shape of your pattern. Lay these edge to edge, right sides inside, and stitch $\frac{1}{2}$″ in along three sides, leaving the bottom end open. Next, turn the case right sides out and firmly sew in the zip across the bottom, turning the edges under so that they do not show.

4. Cut pieces of coloured felt to shapes required—for example, two sixpenny-sized pieces of blue felt for the eyes, and two half-crown-sized pieces of red felt for cheeks—and stick and stitch these into position. Next, cut four ovals for ears,

joining two together to make a pair, with a little lightweight stuffing sandwiched in between, and stitch these firmly to the side seam.

5. Make simple legs and arms; stitch on rug-wool hair, woollen pom-poms, lace edging, gay ribbon, etc., and embroider a mouth and any other features or decorations as required.

As can be seen, the different ways you can make and decorate such cases are numerous. The actual shape, size and method of decorating them depends as much on your own inventiveness as it does on the intended function of the case. When making your pattern use whatever the case is intended to hold only as a rough guide to size, applying your own ideas to the shape and decoration. You could, for instance, equally well make such a case to the shape of a nurse holding a baby, a pineapple, owl, or even a train. And the decorations you choose could, in addition to those we have mentioned, be made from raffia, braids, gaily coloured beads, or indeed anything that takes your fancy. So turn to pages 14, 51 and 92 for other ideas.

Stocking doll. This type of doll is really based on the traditional rag doll, and is usually made from a pair of patterned stockings or knee-length socks, together with oddments of raffia, lace, ribbons, felt cuttings,

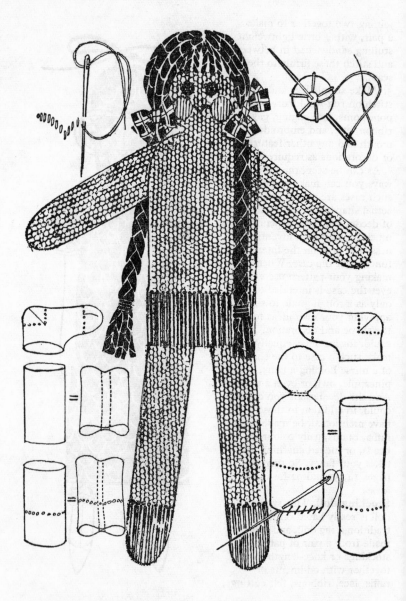

buttons and beads, etc.

The materials required are: a pair of knee-length socks or patterned stockings—old ones will do, as the foot sections will be discarded—small coin-shaped pieces of brightly-coloured felt for the eyes and cheeks, some rug wool for the hair, scarlet embroidery silk for the mouth, and sock-coloured thread for sewing. The filling can be kapok, cut-up stockings, pieces of polythene foam or similar lightweight stuffing.

1. Cut off and discard both foot sections. To make the arms and legs, first turn one sock inside out then stitch two lines, $\frac{1}{2}''$ apart, right down the centre from top to bottom. Next, cut in half across the leg (as shown far right) before cutting between the stitched lines.

Run a gathering stitch $\frac{1}{2}''$ in from welt, and pull tightly, oversewing at seam junction for extra strength. Turn through and fill with pieces of light-weight stuffing. When firm enough turn in $\frac{1}{2}''$ at top and oversew edges together. Repeat this procedure for each limb.

2. To make the body turn the other sock inside out and run a gathering stitch round, and $\frac{1}{2}''$ up from the ankle edge. Pull this tight and oversew several times for strength. Turn to right side and pack in sufficient stuffing to form the head. When this is large enough—approx. 3″ to 4″ from the closed end—

run a gathering stitch around the neck and draw in tightly, stab-stitching for extra strength. Put more stuffing into the rest of the sock to form the body, and when firm enough turn in $\frac{1}{2}''$ at base and oversew edges together.

3. Place oversewn ends of arms on to curved end of shoulders, and stitch into position. Similarly attach the oversewn ends of the legs to the base of the body.

4. Cut two sixpenny-sized pieces of green or blue felt for the eyes and sew into position, as shown top right opposite. Cut two penny-sized pieces of red felt for the cheeks, run-stitching these into position $\frac{1}{8}''$ in from the edge of the face. Embroider a small mouth and nose, as shown top left, before finally making the hair.

5. Cut a number of 6″ lengths of rug wool, or raffia, to make the doll's fringe, and a much larger quantity of 30″ lengths for the plaits. Lay fringe $\frac{1}{2}''$ above the eyes, bringing over and down the back of the head, and stitch across the crown with matching wool. Now bring back pieces forward over the crown to form double fringe. Trim lengths even above eyes.

6. Make the plaits by first folding the 30″ strands in half, so that loops and not cut ends can be attached to the head. Divide each bunch into three equal sections and plait these

together, starting 2″ from the loop, and introducing coloured ribbon into the plaiting if required. Fix ends with a few stitches, an elastic band and a gay ribbon.

Stab-stitch loop-ends on to the centre of the head to cover the fringe seam, and stitch around curve for extra strength with matching wool.

Dolls' clothes. To make a simple dress for the sort of doll described on the previous page, or any similar soft doll, start by laying your doll on to the centre of a piece of stiff brown paper.

1. Draw a simple dress shape around one side of the doll, as shown on the right, marking the centre line between the legs and middle of the neck.

2. Remove doll and fold the paper in half along the centre line of your pattern. Pin through both layers of paper just above the hem, at sleeve end, and just below the shoulder marks before cutting through the double layer to get a full-sized pattern. Check pattern against the doll.

3. For a simple felt dress cut out two identically shaped pieces of coloured felt, using your pattern as a guide, but adding ¼″ seam allowance all round. Lay both pieces together, right sides out, and machine or hand-stitch ¼″ in along both side seams and across shoulders, leaving a 2″ or 3″ gap for the neck opening.

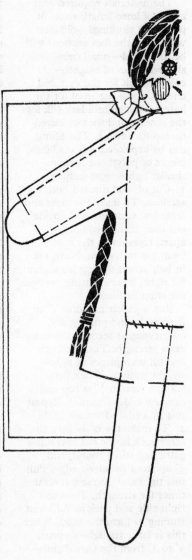

4. Cut 3″ down top centre back and make several button-fastened loops for dressing and undressing, or stitch in a zip.

5. Decorate dress with stuck-on cut-outs of pretty coloured felt pieces, beads, ribbons or embroidered stitches, in a similar way to that already explained for nursery cushions or decorative cases on pages 15 and 25, etc. As felt does not need hemming the dress is now complete; though you could, of course, stick or stitch on a strip of lace around the hem if you wish.

6. For a fabric dress an extra $\frac{1}{2}″$ turning allowance should be added for side and shoulder seams, and an extra 1″ for the hem. The fabric pieces should be stitched inside out and the $\frac{1}{2}″$ seams oversewn or pinked to prevent fraying. The hem should also be neatened, either by turning under and stitching flat, as in normal dressmaking, or by double turning and then machining $\frac{1}{4}″$ from edge and trimming with narrow cotton lace or similar edging.

7. To finish feet of doll, run a gathering stitch $1\frac{1}{2}″$ up from the toes and pull in tightly, stab-stitching through gathering several times for strength. Tie a piece of coloured ribbon over gathering and arrange into a pretty bow. Criss-cross ribbons can also be added.

★ Now make a doll's **carry-cot** as explained on the next page.

Doll's carry-cot. A cane shopping basket, egg basket, or rush Moses basket when lined makes an ideal doll's carry-cot, particularly if some matching sheets and a simple mattress are made to complete the bed.

1. To line the basket a reasonably accurate paper

2. For the side pattern lay the basket on the paper, tilting the basket on to each end while continuing to mark the shape. Cut this rough pattern to the middle curve of each end and fit again on the inside as for the base.

3. Making sure you have left sufficient seam allowance, cut out each piece of fabric. Brightly checked gingham or traditional floral-printed cotton fabric is

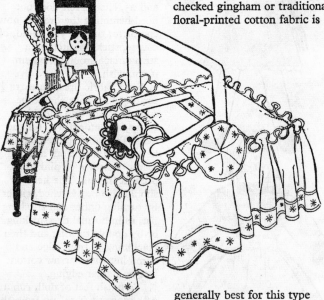

pattern is needed, so using a sheet of cheap brown paper first trace around the outside of the bottom shape, then cut to size. Lay this shape into the basket and tuck the edges into the corners all round, marking the exact size, and re-trim as necessary, but remember to leave on a $\frac{1}{2}''$ seam allowance.

generally best for this type of dolls' carry-cot.

4. For the inside cover cut two side sections, one for the left curve and one for the right, and seam the two ends together. Join your base piece to this by first tacking and then stitching it to the bottom of the side sections along the $\frac{1}{2}''$ allowance marks, easing on slightly.

5. Drop the shape into the basket and attach by tacking 1″ down from the top. Spread the bottom out evenly, and using a long darning needle stab-stitch along the side crevice to hold the fabric permanently to the cane, concealing the stitches as much as possible.

6. To finish the top either turn in ½″ all round and permanently stab-stitch through the gaps between the canework, conceal-

ing the stitches as much as possible, or cut strips of 4″ wide crossway and use these to bind the top edge, turning under and stitching flat along all raw edges.

7. All sorts of frills and flounces can now be added around the top. Simply gather these to size and stitch on as required. The outside of the

basket can also be covered by exactly the same method described for the inside.

Dolls' bedding. Simple dolls' sheets can be made to fit into the carry-cot by cutting out largish rectangles of patterned or coloured fabric. Neaten the edges by rolling and stitching. In a similar way simple dolls' pillows, a soft mattress and bed

covers can also be made to give the carry-cot a complete finish.

A dressing-up doll. This is a more complicated doll to make than the various types already explained on pages 22 and 29, as it involves twelve basic fabric pieces and special trimmings, clothes, underclothes, shoes, socks, bonnet, etc. However, it is great fun to make and should

a

not be too difficult if you have already successfully made several of the simpler toys described earlier in this chapter. It is well worth the extra time and effort as children love to act the role of mother by dressing and undressing a doll, taking her for walks, pretending to feed her, etc.

1. First you need to buy or make the paper pattern required for each section. To make the body, mark out a rectangular shape $8'' \times 5''$, rounding off the corners with the aid of a cocoa tin. For the arms mark out a rectangle $2'' \times 6''$, shaping out a rough thumb shape and then curving into a hand. For the leg pattern mark out a rectangle $2\frac{1}{2}'' \times 8''$, shaping out at one end into a rough chunky foot shape. Finally, for the head mark out a circle $3\frac{1}{2}''$ in diameter but extending the bottom edge into a neck $1\frac{1}{2}''$ wide by $1''$ long.

2. Cut out pattern pieces to be used as a template for cutting the fabric, remembering however that no turning allowances have been made. Using a fairly hard pencil trace around each pattern piece on to the back of cotton body fabric, repeating the body and head twice, and the arms and legs twice one way and twice reversing the pattern.

3. Cut out the cotton fabric, allowing $\frac{1}{2}''$ turning on body and head but only $\frac{1}{4}''$ for arms and legs. Place right sides of matching pieces face to face and stitch along pencil lines,

34

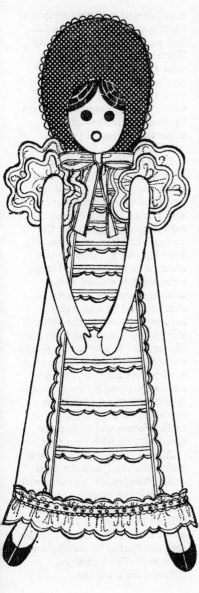

leaving body and head sections open at neck edge, and arm and leg sections open at straight ends.

4. Turn each section through gap so right side is outside. Stuff with kapok or other inexpensive lightweight stuffing. When arms and legs have sufficient filling turn in raw ends and oversew edges together. Turn in raw edges of body gap, but do not oversew.

5. At the neck end of head insert a 6″ length of ½″ wooden dowelling, or something similar, so that 3″ of it go up into the head. Next, place neck inside the body gap so bottom of wood goes 3″ into chest and then sew neck edge of the body to neck edge of the head, adding a little extra stuffing if required. The wood thus acts as a neck support. Sew arms and legs into position just clear of rounded corners.

6. For the face and hair either follow the simple instructions explained on page 29, or purchase a ready-made fabric face at your local hobby shop or the notions counter of a large store.

7. Make several dresses to fit your doll as explained on page 30; also make some simple under-clothes, tights, socks, and even felt or leather shoes, etc., as shown on the left.

Decorative dolls. Many other kinds of dolls and doll puppets can be designed and made by those who like to experiment, particularly if some experience

35

has already been gained through making several traditional ones. As we have explained earlier, there are no hard and fast rules governing the sewing techniques you may use. The only criterion is whether your children and you like the particular doll or toy you have made.

When you are thinking of starting a new doll, don't just remake the same version again and again simply because it has proved successful. Spend a little time looking at soft dolls in your local store or toyshop; also look at the animated puppets to get some different ideas, and in particular note how the arms and legs can be made so that they move about quite freely. Look at the doll's clothes for design ideas and quick ways of making them. Spend a little time browsing through the shop's fabric remnants for new or different sorts of trimmings. Buy a small selection of those you specially like, not for any doll in particular but simply to have on hand for when you feel like making something new.

Start a scrap-book for noting down your various ideas and observations on interesting surface treatments, new things to make, different materials to use, etc., as novelty is what makes sewing fun. If you read an article in a newspaper or magazine showing how to make something you might like to tackle one day, cut it out,

together with any photographs of ideas you think are successful, and paste these into your book. Then whenever you have the urge to create something new you will only have to refer to your book to find a wealth of ideas. Such a scrap-book, if kept up-to-date, will become as important to you as your scissors or pins.

If there are several children to make for, see if you can get them interested in producing a puppet show. Try making a selection of glove puppets, explained on page 16, for the younger children, and several jumping-jack puppets for the older ones, see page 20. Design your puppets around some favourite book illustrations so that you will be reasonably accurate with Alice, the White Rabbit, the Queen, and the Mad Hatter, etc. If you can then read the story while the children enact it with their puppets, or if you have a long-playing record with both the story and music, as explained on page 20, then endless hours will be happily spent playing with your toys.

As you can see, your scope is quite unlimited, and the most delightful toys can be made with the maximum of ease and pleasure and the minimum of skill and trouble. So remember never to let your sewing become dull and boring by continuous repetition. Try something different for a change.

2. Party Clothes and Things

In this chapter we shall explain some of the simplest ways of making various sorts of party things, from party bibs and aprons to fancy dress ideas and presents. Many of the designs and instructions are only intended to be used as a basis from which to work and develop further designs of your own, and we hope they will encourage you to attempt making all sorts of things you have never tried before. With this in mind, and remembering that there are

really no hard and fast rules to worry about, you should be able to regard your sewing as something to be done just for the fun of it and for the satisfaction and enjoyment of seeing a finished article which you have created. Your efforts will always be an exciting challenge rather than an exacting task, if you make a point of trying your hand at new things, made in different ways, and avoiding all the confusing and off-putting jargon of traditional craft techniques. You cannot do better than start by making something bold and bright and in the simplest way possible, for it is only by taking the plunge that sewing becomes really exciting and fun to do.

Party bibs. Materials required: a square of terry towelling—a flannel or small hand-towel will do—coloured bias binding, ribbon and sewing cotton to match, and pieces of coloured felt or fabric.

1. Mark out a 9″ square or size and shape of bib required on to a piece of stiff wrapping paper, rounding off the corners with chalk. Machine stitch around this line and again just inside it to prevent unravelling when cutting out and making up.

3. Cut out fabric $\frac{1}{8}$″ away from outside machine line. Using the simple sewing machine binding foot, stitch on the bias binding round all the raw edges, except the neck edge. Next bind the neck edge by hand, if you find

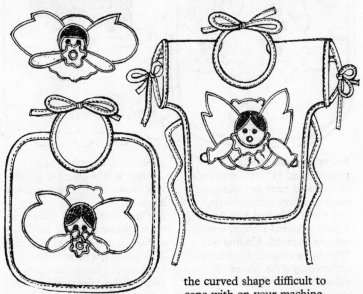

the aid of a cocoa tin. In the exact centre of the top edge place the cocoa tin so that it comes just over half way on to the bib shape, tracing this curve to form the neckline.

2. Cut out your paper pattern and using it as a template mark your fabric to this shape with a normal pencil or dressmakers'

the curved shape difficult to cope with on your machine, leaving a $\frac{1}{2}$″ of binding at each end. Tuck this binding to back of bib and catch-stitch down.

4. As this is a party bib cut a yard of pretty ribbon into two pieces and sew on to each side of the neck for tying into an attractive bow. Finally add some decorations as required, coloured cut-outs, embroidery etc.

Party aprons. Materials required: an 11″ × 16″ rectangle of coloured terry towelling, sail-cloth or heavy cotton fabric, 2–3 yards coloured bias binding, 1 yard coloured ribbon, sewing cottons to match binding and ribbon, various coloured raffia or embroidery silks, pieces of coloured felt or fabric, and a simple doll or other novelty to fit in a pocket.

1. Mark out your rectangle on to a piece of stiff wrapping paper, rounding off the two shorter sides with the aid of a saucer. At the top 11″ end measure and mark exactly 2″ in from each side and then measure and mark 6″ down the 16″ sides, drawing an inward

curve to connect the rough armhole marks together in the way shown for the party aprons opposite.

2. Cut out the paper pattern and try it against the child for size and shape, adjusting as necessary. Now using it as a template mark on the fabric the exact shape with a normal pencil or dressmakers' chalk. Machine stitch around this shape and again ⅛″ inside it to prevent unravelling.

3. Cut out the fabric ⅛″ away from the outside machine line. Using the simple sewing machine binding foot, or the method shown for binding on page 50, stitch on the bias strip round all the raw edges making a neat

40

join at the corners.

4. Cut the coloured ribbon in half and stitch one end of each to apron waist at bottom of armhole shaping. Taking the right-hand ribbon pass it diagonally across the back to the top left corner, and taking the left-hand ribbon pass it likewise to the top right corner—as illustrated below—adjusting the length of both according to the child's size before fastening to binding with a press stud. Alternatively sew an extra ½ yard across the top to form a normal neck band—as shown on the left—using the waist ribbons to tie in a traditional back bow.

5. To decorate the apron cut out various coloured felt shapes, sticking then stitching them into position. Add embroidery details, raffia work, beads, bits and bobs or any other novelties you like.

6. If you wish to make a pocket in the apron try designing one with a difference, making it flower-shaped, chimney-shaped, pram-shaped or even a sock-shaped pocket as below.

7. Finally, make a simple doll to fit into the apron pocket by following the instructions given in chapter 1, page 23, etc. As you can see this sort of apron can be great fun, particularly at Christmas time with a Father Christmas in a felt stocking or stuck in the chimney. But it would be equally appealing if it

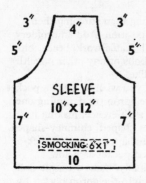

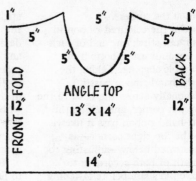

was a felt rabbit, clown, or a pair of glove puppets; as there are no rules try your hand at making one of your own ideas, just for fun.

Angle top. Materials required: 1 yard of fabric, 1½ yards of 1″ wide lace edging, stitching cotton, 1 yard of ¼″ elastic, coloured embroidery threads, a sheet of plain wrapping paper.
1. Mark out in pencil on to the wrapping paper three rectangles: one measuring 13″ × 14″ for the body pattern, one measuring 10″ × 12″ for the raglan sleeves, and one 22½″ × 12″ for the pants.
2. Following the pattern

diagrams above and below shape the rectangular pieces as shown, checking the shapes and measurements very carefully before finally cutting out.
3. Using dressmakers' chalk mark on to the fabric the shape of the paper pattern pieces, remembering to double the body pattern over when marking so as to avoid a centre front seam. Also remember to mark out two sleeves. Cut around these shapes.

Making top. 1. Using the French seam method of sewing, join the 7″ sleeve seams by machining first ¼″ on right side, trimming to ⅛″, then another ¼″ on wrong

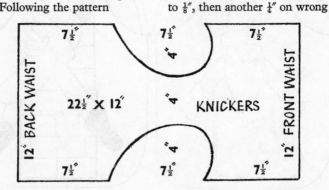

42

side, as shown on page 48, dia. C. Again using a French seam set in the sleeves.

2. Make six parallel lines of hand-gathered stitching at $\frac{1}{4}''$ intervals around the neck, gathering up to 9″, stitching on and neatening a narrow crossway binding; see page 50, dia. 3.

3. Now is the time to check both the body and sleeve lengths if this is necessary remembering that a $\frac{1}{2}''$ allowance is needed for hem turnback.

gather, then smock, as for neck.

5. Using the method shown on page 50 attach the 1″ edging lace around the hem and sleeve edges, before finally embroidering some flowers just above the hem, sewing on a press stud $\frac{1}{2}''$ from the top of back opening and three others at 2″ intervals down the back.

Making knickers. 1. Using the run and fell seam method shown on page 113 sew the $7\frac{1}{2}''$ side seams together.

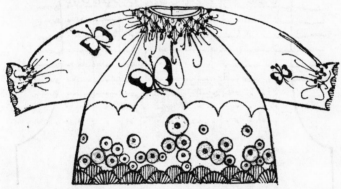

Neaten sleeve hem by first turning up $\frac{1}{4}''$ and stitching flat, then turning up another $\frac{1}{4}''$ and stitching flat so as to bind in the raw edges. Neaten back edges in the same way and then the hem.

4. Having gathered and bound the neck the next thing is to smock stitch the evenly gathered folds as explained on page 45. One inch from the bottom of the sleeves mark out a 6″ × 1″ rectangle—as shown on the pattern diagram top left—and

2. Turn in $\frac{1}{4}''$ around waist line and stitch flat. Next turn in $\frac{3}{4}''$ and again stitch flat $\frac{1}{8}''$ away from both inside and outside edges.

3. Using the leg finishing method shown on page 113 face out and neaten the leg openings. Cut two 9″ lengths of elastic and slot one into each leg facing, overlapping the ends and stitching through to hold together.

4. Slot the remaining elastic through waistband, again

overlapping the ends and joining together securely. Decorate the knickers in the same way as the top if required, adding lace edge, embroidery etc.

Smocking. Smocking is a very attractive traditional form of surface decoration used to hold fullness together neatly and evenly. Naturally the amount of smocking used varies with the changing fashion trends, but as a general rule wherever fullness is

These transfers can be purchased at most needlework shops and notion counters. Iron the transfer on to the wrong side of the material, allowing about three times the width of fabric to the width the finished smocking is to be. The gathering should also be done on the wrong side, taking up each dot with a small piece of the material—as shown below— securing the threads at the

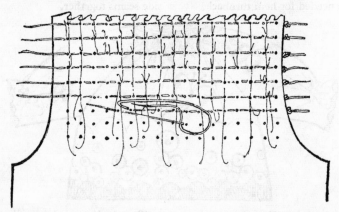

used on children's clothes the addition of smocking gives it an interesting and decorative appearance.

Evenness in smocking is the key to success, and this depends almost entirely upon the regularity of the gathering, which must be done before the actual decorative stitching.

First, decide the depth and width the smocking is to be; then cut from a smocking transfer the depth of dots required.

beginning of each row with a knot. When all the rows have been run, draw up the thread sufficiently tight to allow the pleats to be easily worked, and secure by knotting together.

An alternative, but inferior, method is to iron the transfer dots on to the right side and omit the gathering, but this is only suitable for very small areas. For ease of diagrammatical explanation this method is illustrated, but once the stitches have been practised the gathering method is far better.

Cable smocking. Working from left to right over a line of dots ¼″ apart bring thread up through first dot, pick up next dot with thread above the needle and draw up. Pick up next dot with thread below the needle and draw up as shown in diagram A below; repeat with thread alternating above and below the needle right along the line.

above needle pick up dot below previous one—number 4. With thread below needle pick up next dot which will be number 1 of next complete stitch. Repeat this procedure along the line before stitching second and third lines.

Finally, remove the gathering stitches and the smocking will then be able to give slightly in movement.

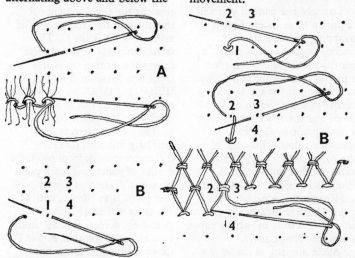

A

B

2 3
4

B

2 3
1 4

2 3
1 4

Honeycombing. Working from left to right over alternating lines of ¼″ dots, bring the needle out of a dot as in diagram B. With thread below needle pick up the next dot—number 1— draw together, pick up dot above last dot—number 2—draw up. With thread above the needle pick up next dot—number 3— draw together. With thread still

Shirring. This is another way of adapting fullness in a small decorative garment. Shirring is achieved by winding a specially made elastic thread on to the bobbin of a sewing machine and stitching in parallel lines over the required area. The area covered automatically pleats in a decorative way and will have the all important suppleness in movement.

45

Petticoat pattern. On the page opposite is shown a draft for a simple petticoat which can be made for a little girl of between 2 and 3 years old. If this pattern is not quite right for size, then simply by reducing the width and length slightly to make it smaller or increasing them slightly to make it larger, you will find it will cover most sizes to fit from 1 to 4-year-olds.

To make the pattern you will require a large sheet of plain wrapping paper, a sheet of tracing or greaseproof paper, a pencil, rubber and ruler, plus a pair of scissors for cutting out.

1. Starting at the top left corner of the paper measure 2½″ down and mark accurately with a dot—point A. Continue measuring down this edge of the paper another 15½″, and mark another dot—point B. From here measure 8″ at right angles across the paper to give point C. Next measure 3″ down from A and then 6½″ across paper from here for point D.

2. Again starting at the very top left corner measure 2½″ along the top edge and mark point E. Continue measuring another 2″ but this time marking dot ½″ away from the edge for point F. Using your ruler and pencil connect points E to F, B to C, and C to D with accurate straight lines.

3. Using tracing paper, or a sheet of see-through greaseproof paper, trace the front neckline—

shown actual size by the double broken line at the top of the draft opposite. Place this tracing on top of your pattern so that it matches E exactly, and that centre front fold lines also match. Mark neckline through tracing on to pattern.

4. Trace armhole shape from draft pattern, following broken line accurately, as for neck shape. Trace on to pattern, making sure that the top point matches F exactly, and that the bottom of armhole is on point D. The front pattern is now complete except for writing on centre front line between A and B, 'FRONT FOLD' as shown. Do remember that this is to be cut double on the fabric fold.

5. The back pattern is made similarly but with these differences: work from top right corner of paper and mark point A only 1″ from that corner and point B 17″ down, with C 8″ across and D 4½″ down from A and 6½″ across. E is 2½″ from corner, and F another 2″ but ½″ down from edge. Draw lines connecting E to F, B to C, and C to D.

6. Trace back neck following double dash-and-dot line and back armhole, marking these on to the pattern as previously explained.

7. Shoulder and side seam allowances of ½″ have been included in this pattern, together with a ½″ hem neatening allowance. As the neckline and

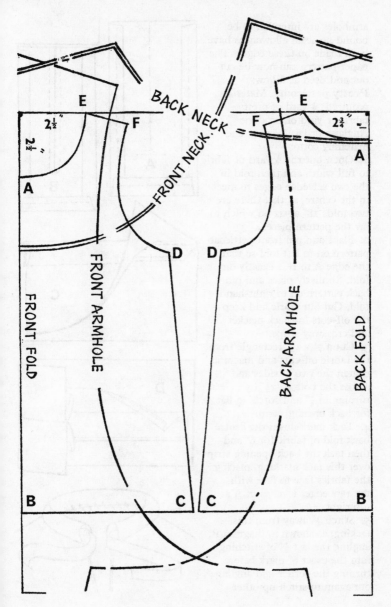

2½"

2¼"

E

F

A

BACK NECK.

FRONT NECK.

E

F

2¾"

A

FRONT FOLD

FRONT ARMHOLE

D

D

BACK ARMHOLE

BACK FOLD

B

C

C

B

armholes are intended to be bound no seam allowances have been made on these edges. The paper pattern can now be cut out and used as follows:

Pretty petticoats. Materials required: $\frac{1}{2}$ yard of pretty **fabric**, 1 yard of Broderie Anglaise or lace edging, and matching cotton.

1. Open out the $\frac{1}{2}$ yard of fabric to full width and then fold in the two selvedge edges to meet in the centre, so that there are two folds 18″ apart on which to lay the pattern pieces.

2. Place and pin front petticoat pattern on to left fold so that the edge A to B is exactly on fold. Similarly place and pin back pattern on to right-hand fold. Cut out fabric and keep the off-cuts for back placket and crossway strips.

3. Cut a 7″ × 2½″ rectangle from the fabric off-cuts and machine neaten the two 7″ sides and across the bottom 2½″ by turning in ¼″ and stitching flat for back opening strip.

4. Tack mark down the centre back fold of fabric for 6″ and then tack the back opening strip over this tack marking, placing the fabrics face to face with top raw edges level as in A at top right.

5. Stitch ¼″ away from this tacking, as shown in diagram B, angling the last ½″ of stitching into the exact 6″ mark before turning the corner and angling out again to stitch up other

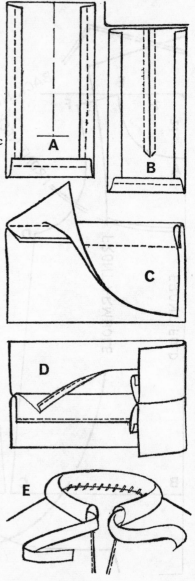

48

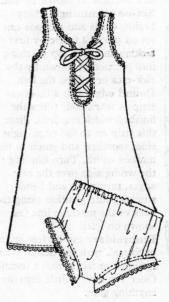

side. Cut in between the stitching right up to bottom 6" mark and turn through.

6. Iron slit edge flat and then stitch through fold $\frac{1}{4}$" away from edge and again $\frac{1}{8}$" away from rectangle edges to keep opening and facing flat and firm.

7. Stitch together front and back shoulder seams using either the flat fell method—shown on page 113—a french seam as in diagram C and explained on page 42, or by making a normal flat open seam as in diagram D. Similarly join the side seams together.

8. Using the larger pieces of fabric off-cuts, make 4 ft. of 1" wide crossway binding for the armholes, using binding method shown on page 50; alternatively you could use ordinary bias binding and stitch it on with the aid of the special binding foot attachment sold with most sewing machines.

9. Bind the petticoat neck in a similar way, tucking back inside $\frac{1}{2}$" of turning at each end so that an 18" length of $\frac{1}{4}$" ribbon can be slotted through to form a drawstring, as shown in diagram E.

10. Neaten hem by turning under first $\frac{1}{4}$" and stitching flat and then another $\frac{1}{4}$" which should again be stitched flat before finally hand sewing on some lace edging or Broderie Anglaise, as shown on page 50.

Pretty knickers. Using $\frac{1}{8}$ yard of fabric and 1 yard of $\frac{1}{4}$" or $\frac{3}{8}$"

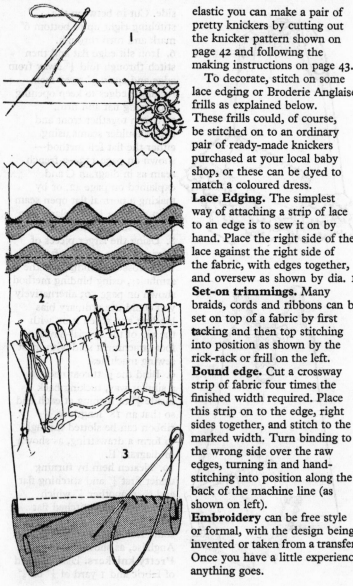

elastic you can make a pair of pretty knickers by cutting out the knicker pattern shown on page 42 and following the making instructions on page 43.

To decorate, stitch on some lace edging or Broderie Anglaise frills as explained below. These frills could, of course, be stitched on to an ordinary pair of ready-made knickers purchased at your local baby shop, or these can be dyed to match a coloured dress.

Lace Edging. The simplest way of attaching a strip of lace to an edge is to sew it on by hand. Place the right side of the lace against the right side of the fabric, with edges together, and oversew as shown by dia. 1.

Set-on trimmings. Many braids, cords and ribbons can be set on top of a fabric by first tacking and then top stitching into position as shown by the rick-rack or frill on the left.

Bound edge. Cut a crossway strip of fabric four times the finished width required. Place this strip on to the edge, right sides together, and stitch to the marked width. Turn binding to the wrong side over the raw edges, turning in and hand-stitching into position along the back of the machine line (as shown on left).

Embroidery can be free style or formal, with the design being invented or taken from a transfer. Once you have a little experience anything goes.

Traditionalists use skeins of embroidery cotton when working but it can be great fun to substitute these with knitting wools, raffia, strands of leather or plastic, ribbons, cord and braid, or even coloured string.

Just a few of the many stitches which can be used are illustrated here and on pages 92–95 but many more can easily be learnt by those who are interested.

1. **Stem stitch.** Make regular, slightly slanting stitches along the line of the design, with the top thread always emerging at top left side of the previous one.

2. **Couching.** Lay a thick coloured thread along the line of design and with another thread loop it down at regular intervals

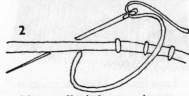

with a small stitch across it.

3. **Chain stitch.** Make a stitch on the right-hand side of the design, catching loop down with left thumb. Insert the needle just below where it last emerged, and bring the point out ¼″ away so that the thread passes under the point to form

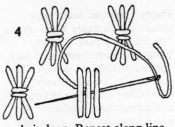

a chain loop. Repeat along line as shown below, diagram 3.

4. **Sheaf stitch.** First work three vertical stitches, then tie across the centre of these with two over-casting stitches. The over-casting should be free

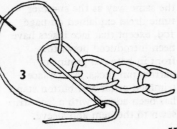

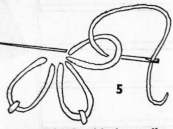

from the fabric with the needle only entering it again to complete the tie.

5. **Daisy stitch.** Work this stitch in the same way as chain stitch, but fasten each loop with a small stitch as shown above and radiate from a central point to form daisy shape.

51

Party Dresses. Many pretty things can be made when sewing for children's parties, from party dresses trimmed with lace edging, decorative insets, tucks and gathers, smocking and embroidery to frilly knickers and petticoats as explained on pages 42 to 49, and of course many fancy dress party clothes such as shown on pages 56–59.

Boy's designs can also be made for most party occasions, the designs ranging from the satin shirt with velvet trousers shown opposite to all sorts of fancy dress ideas shown on pages 56 to 59. These designs can be decorated with tucks and pleats, jewelled buttons and cuff-links, embroidered waistcoats, crochet ties and fancy belts, etc.

The simple little party dress shown above is made in much the same way as the summer tunic dress explained on page 109, except that lace insets have been introduced down the front in between groups of narrow pin tucks. Also a lace trimmed collar and button stand has been added, with a lace strip sewn to the hem and sleeve.

Lace insets. Mark the position with coloured tackings on to the fabric, keeping the edges on the exact grain line. Cut a strip of the decorative insert to the length required and then cut the fabric exactly between the coloured tacking lines. Fold under the surplus material edge stitching the fold on to the inset strip.

Pin tucks. Many twin-needle machines make automatic pin tucks which can also be raised and corded, or they can be made on most other sewing machines by accurately top stitching $\frac{1}{8}''$ away from a folded edge of fabric. Accuracy when marking is essential as each tuck must be on the exact grain, creasing along this mark before

As it is almost impossible to judge exactly how much extra material is required for a particular tucked area it is wisest to cut the material much larger than the pattern, tucking as required before trimming accurately to shape.

Decorative buttons. These can generally be purchased in most shops or stores in a wide

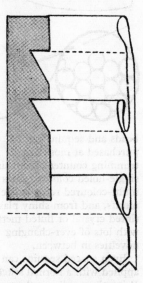

stitching close to the folded edge.

Tuck making. As explained for pin tucks it is essential for each tuck to be made on the exact grain. The only difference is that the stitching is away from the folded edge of a tuck, usually measuring between $\frac{1}{4}''$ to $\frac{1}{2}''$, using a notched cardboard tuck guide as illustrated above right.

variety of sizes and interesting designs, ranging from shaped metal, coloured cording, moulded glass and plastics, to jewelled and sequinned buttons. Similarly decorative buckles are also available, or button and buckle sets can easily be made as explained on the next page.

Beads and sequins. A seemingly unending variety of

53

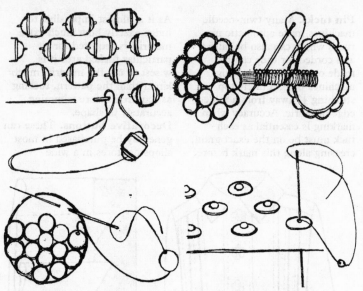

beads and sequins can be purchased at most large trimming counters, from simple single-holed coloured discs to multi-coloured ready-made motifs, and from shiny plastic to tinted crystal or fluted metal, with lots of ever-changing novelties in between.

Even spaced sequins can be applied with a normal stitch. Bring the needle up through the fabric and centre hole of the sequin, taking stitch over the edge and back through the fabric. Bring the needle up again through the fabric and another sequin ⅛″ away and take another stitch over the edge, repeating all over the design. Another way is to sew on single sequins with the aid of a

small coloured bead. Using a very fine needle bring it up through the fabric and sequin as before. Pass the needle through the centre hole of a small bead and then take the needle over and back through the hole and material, repeating to complete your pattern. If many sequins are being applied a safety knot should be made after each ten or twelve in case the thread breaks during wear.

Evenly spaced beads are applied with a normal stitch, as can be seen by the illustrations above, whilst very small beads can be attached by threading six or seven on to the needle at each stitch; even an inch of beads can be attached in this way if required.

Beaded buttons. Many designs of decorative buttons can be bought ready-made, and many more can be made by twisting, looping, twirling, plaiting or knotting cord, raffia, rouleaux, dyed string, pipe cleaners, or even electrical wire covering, and incorporating beads, sequins, motifs, dried seeds, plastic pieces, etc. Simply try several out and if they are successful blind-stab-stitch through several times to hold firm and either work a bar across the back to act as a shank or sew on to a covered button, as shown on the left.

Cuff-link buttons are made by linking two pairs of decorative buttons together with several strands of silk buttonhole twist and then loop-stitching over these to form a firm chain.

Decorative buckles are made by twisting with cord, covering with beads and innumerable other ways, to match buttons, or cuff-links, or to use on their own. Try making a simple one first, and then anything goes.

Beaded bracelets or simple necklaces can be made by threading beads on to shirring elastic or beading thread. The designs can be as simple as those shown below, or the threading can be done in a more complex way—as shown on the left—for making belts, bracelets, watch straps, neck ties, or even bright shiny beaded bags.

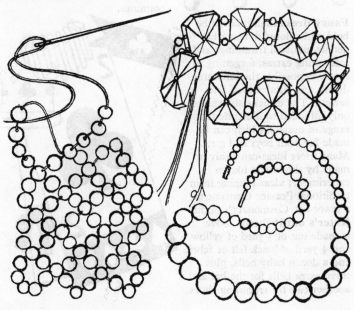

55

To make the basic Jester pattern first mark-out the simple tunic pattern shown on page 108, but instead of drawing a straight hem mark an evenly jagged hem as shown on the left, and draw a line across the pattern just above the waist.

Next cut out four 9″ squares of yellow felt or fabric and four of black. Using two yellow and two black squares stitch them together to form a $17\frac{1}{2}″ \times 17\frac{1}{2}″$ checkerboard square, then join the other four in a similar way. Now simply continue making the dress in the easiest possible way, marking out the shape with the waist pattern line and centre lines placed on the yellow-black seamings.

Fancy dress ideas should be bold and colourful, using big details, unusual trimmings and interesting extras, forgetting as much as possible the intricate details and subtleties of fine sewing. The designs shown are only intended to illustrate the range of designs which can be made for both boys and girls. Many more ideas can easily be made by those who like to experiment; ideas ranging from traditional Peasant Costume to a space-age Cosmonaut's outfit. **Jester's outfit** shown above is made out of $\frac{1}{2}$ yard of yellow and $\frac{1}{2}$ yard of black felt or fabric and a dozen baby bells, plus three extra bells for the hat and another two for trimming shoes.

If felt has been used then the hem can be cut to shape without any finishing, but if the tunic has been made of fabric then face back ¼″ with bias binding. Similarly for the jagged collar, which can be cut to any size and shape you like.

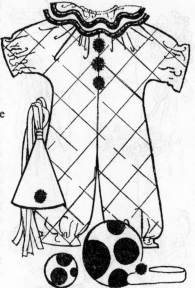

To make the hat, first measure round the child's head and then experiment with brown paper, using the head measurement as a guide for size. When you have discovered the most successful shape use your brown paper pattern to cut out the felt, remembering to add on ½″ all round for turnings.

Finally sew on the bells to each jagged corner and a bow and bell on each shoe.

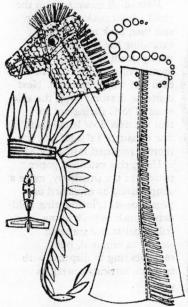

Cowboys and Indians. First trim a pair of ordinary denim jeans with a 2½″ wide strip of coloured felt which has been snipped every ¼″ to make a deep fringe. This felt fringed strip should be stuck on to the side seams with UHU glue and then hand stitched for extra strength. Next make a hobby horse as explained on page 17.

Make the Indian head-dress out of a 2″ wide strip of felt sewn to fit on to the head and then trimmed with real feathers, or feathers made from 8″ × 2″ felt feather shapes slotted with pipe cleaners, adding two feathered ribbons at the back for a Warrior Chief.

57

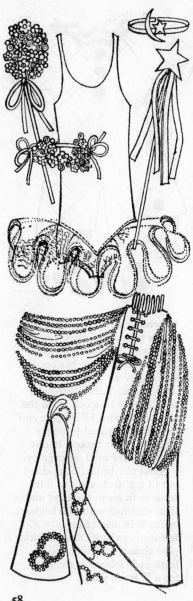

Fairy dresses can vary from the brief design shown above left to the more elaborate long dress shown below. But whichever dress you prefer to make remember that the dress itself is only half the design, and that the head-dress, shoes and magic wand are also very important.

To make the little Sugar Plum Fairy design you will find it easiest to adapt a simple ballet leotard or dyed singlet and knickers, adding circular cut frills of net around the hip line. For the more elaborate Fairy Godmother's dress a paper pattern will be required, cut on the lines of that shown on page 108, but of a more flared shape extended to reach the floor.

First of all measure from the child's front neck to the floor and then back neck to floor, extending the line A to B on your pattern to those measurements plus 2″ extra for hem and seam allowance. Next continue drawing down the side seam D to C flaring out so that the new floor length hem line measures 14″ × 16″ or even more if required instead of 8½″.

Using this extended paper pattern in the usual way, make a simple dress as explained on pages 109–111, introducing bold details such as neck lacing, frilled collar and gathered sleeves as required, but remembering to dispense with as much intricate sewing as possible.

Before going to a lot of trouble to make the head-dress, shoes and magic wand, spend a little time experimenting with coloured paper, tinsel, beads, ribbons and UHU glue to see what can be easily achieved, sticking some extras on to the dress if required.

As with all childrens' fancy dress, novelty, bold colours and interesting design are much more

design details, unusual trimming and interesting extras. As there is such a variety to choose from only a brief explanation of what to make will be given here, the various things being made as explained earlier.

For instance the felt waistcoat is stuck and stitched together, but the front, hem, and armholes edges left raw and then

important than beautiful sewing, so provided the dress doesn't fall to pieces, stick rather than stitch as much as possible.

Peasant costumes can be made in many ways out of prettily patterned fabrics combined with brightly coloured felts, decorated with bold embroideries or smocking, and using big

decorated with bold embroidery as shown on pages 51 and 94, beading as shown on page 54, and braiding as explained on pages 92 and 93. Similarly the circular skirt, smocked blouse or Broderie Anglaise cap and apron should be made by the quickest and simplest method.

59

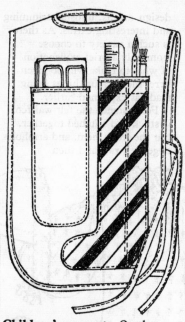

this type of tabard apron are: ½ yard of gaily-coloured sturdy fabric—which should be semi-waterproof—some pieces of contrasting materials for pockets, webbing or tape for pencil loops or appliqué numbers, coloured bias binding for edge finishing, and 1½ yards of ribbon for the side ties—plus a sheet of plain wrapping paper and pencil for making the basic pattern.

1. To cut a tabard pattern simply draw out the petticoat pattern explained on page 46, but reducing the front measurement A to B to 14″ and hem B to C to 6½″, rounding off corner C with the aid of a saucer. In the same way modify the back A to B to 15½″ and B to C to 6½″.

Children's presents. On the following eight pages are shown a few ideas for presents to make for children. These are only intended to illustrate the sort of things which can be made easily, many other ideas in this book being equally suitable— as indeed are the many more ideas you may have seen in magazines, newspapers, other books, or your local toy shop.

Play aprons. The two shown on the top left and top right are based on the tabard type of apron, designed to protect the front and back of children's clothes when playing with crayons, chalks, paint etc.

The materials required for

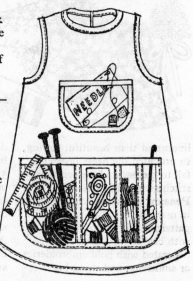

2. Now cut out the paper pattern, and remembering to put the centre front and centre back to the double folded fabric, as on page 48, then cut out fabric. Next stitch out the back opening as also explained on page 48.

3. Join the front and back shoulder seams together using a normal flat open seam, and then bind the neck and armholes in coloured bias binding as for a normal apron or bib, shown on pages 39, 50.

4. Cut out various pocket shapes in paper to see which design you prefer and then cut these shapes out in the contrasting fabric pieces, possibly see-through polythene or coloured felt. Bind the pocket

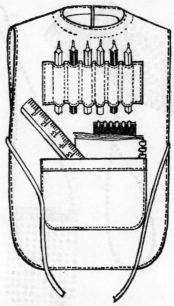

edges in bias binding and then top stitch them into position.

5. Do not join the side seams together, instead either turn under ¼″ and stitch flat or bind in bias strip, continuing down one side across hem and around other side all in one go.

6. Finally, cut 1½ yards of ribbon into four equal pieces and sew one piece on to the bottom of each armhole before finishing the back neck with a simple hook and eye or button and loop.

* **Play dresses** are made in a similar way to the play aprons but are based on the pattern and making instructions given on pages 108 to 112.

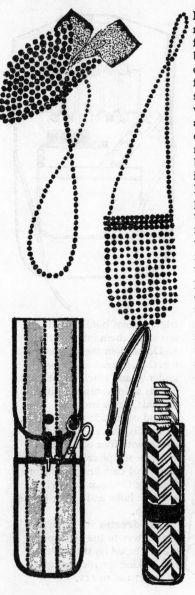

Play cases and bags can be made in many shapes and sizes, from small comb cases to beaded shoulder bags, and out of a wide variety of materials, from corduroy, cotton rep and sailcloth to leather and plastic, with lots of beads and trimmings added for interest. Just two examples are explained but lots more cases and bags can easily be made by improvising on the instructions given.

Pencil case. Cut a paper pattern 10″ square. Write on top edge 'Flap End' and then round off the two flap corners with the aid of a cocoa tin.

2. Cut a piece of firm fabric the exact size of the paper pattern, turning in a ½″ on the opposite edge to the flap and stitching flat.

3. Using the simple sewing machine binding foot attachment, stitch on coloured bias binding all round the three remaining edges, starting at the right-hand corner and finishing at the left corner in one continuous line.

4. Measure 2½″ down from the flap edge and mark a line. Now fold opposite straight edge up to this line, stitching through both 3½″ side seams ¼″ in from butted edges.

5. Fold flap down and attach a fastening, using either large dressmakers' press studs, hammered-on snap fasteners, a strap and buckle, or button and tab, etc., adding extra loops, rings, handles or straps

as required.

Beaded bag. I. To make a round beaded bag cut two circles of stiffish fabric using a saucer or plate as a guide.

2. With the normal sewing machine binding foot attachment, stitch on some matching coloured bias binding around each circular piece.

3. Sew on a pattern of beads and sequins as required, following the general beading instructions given on page 54, sticking on the beads in between with UHU glue. Coloured cut-outs of felt or plastic could also be stuck and stitched on as required.

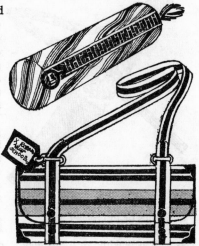

4. Cut two circles of thin felt $\frac{1}{8}''$ smaller than your fabric pieces and with UHU glue stick these carefully on to the back of your main pieces to cover stitches, making sure that the edges are firmly attached but not letting the glue go on to the fabric surface.

5. The two circles can now be sewn together around $\frac{2}{3}$ of the bag, but if the beads are near the edge then the stitching must be done by hand, stab-stitching right through both circles every $\frac{1}{8}''$ with silk buttonhole twist, rather like traditional saddle stitching; the top $\frac{1}{3}$ is left unstitched to form the opening.

6. Sew in a 4″ to 6″ zip and then add a beaded handle, or a handle made from a decorative cord or braid.

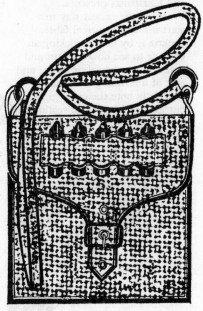

63

Crochet. Those who can already crochet will find the simple tie shown on the left an easy task, while those who have never crocheted need only a little practice to see how easy crochet really is, for it is simply a matter of looping threads together with the aid of a hook. To start crocheting it is probably best to buy from your local stockist a simple pattern, crochet hook and thread, and once you start you will find you can make up your own designs as you go along.

Neckties in a wide variety of fabrics or in crochet and knitting can be great fun to do, as well as making ideal birthday and Christmas presents. Probably the easiest way to start making a normal fabric necktie is by first unpicking an old one to see how it is cut and made. Note the fabric shape and sort of interlining used, and especially note the cross-grain cutting, half-way inset sections, end finishing and hand-stitched centre back lap seaming. Simply copy in the fabric of your choice.

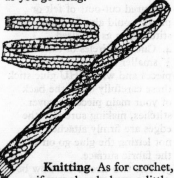

Knitting. As for crochet, if you already have a little experience it will be quite easy to knit a simple tie like the one shown above, while those who have never knitted will soon discover how simple it really can be. The complete beginner should start by buying a beginner's pattern, some medium-sized needles and a little coloured wool, and try knitting some ties for the next batch of presents. Once you have mastered the basic pattern don't be tempted to just

64

repeat it, but improvise on the instructions to change the design each time.

Headgear can also be sewn, crocheted or knitted as can be seen from the three designs shown on this page.

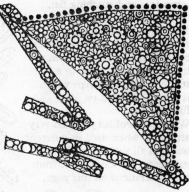

The easiest design to start with is a simple head square, which requires a 30″–36″ square of soft fabric for an adult size, or between 20″ and 30″ for children or young teenagers. This square should be double rolled round the edges, using the

Fold the 16″ square diagonally across, with the right sides inside, and pin the fabric edges together accurately before stitching from fold to fold ¼″ from edges, and leaving a 2″ gap in the centre of one side. Turn the fabric through this gap so that the right side is now outside, and slip-stitch together. Cut the ribbon in half and attach one piece to each folded corner. Next stitch on the lace edging round the seamed sides, folding the little extra lace to the back of the ribbon to cover all the

simple machine foot edge turning attachment.

An alternative method, and one which not only requires less fabric but is more decorative, is shown, top right. For this design a 12″–16″ square of pretty soft cotton or silky fabric is required, together with a yard of cotton lace edging and coloured ribbon.

raw edges and stitching flat.

Also shown are just three crochet and knitted hats, ranging from a simple crocheted beret, and another one with a bold rib knitted peak, to a striped stocking design which is circular knitted on four needles.

Wool embroidery can be very attractive when used in different ways on all sorts of ready-made garments. As you will see from the illustrations on this page,

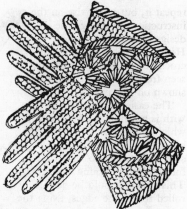

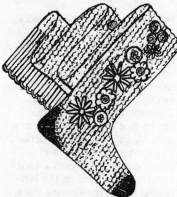

you can easily add a few very decorative flowers on to a pair of bought knee socks or winter fancy-knit stockings, and these could be teamed with gloves, berets, scarves or even a sweater and cardigan.

Just a few of the many stitches used in this type of embroidery are shown on page 51, with many more being easily learnt from the numerous embroidery pamphlets and design transfers on sale at most

sewing shops. As well as the great variety of stitches, there are also a great number of different thread combinations which can be used in addition to coloured wools, including string, russia braids, strips of leather and plastic, beads, ribbons and many, many novelties. Always be on the look-out for new ideas: this is partly what makes sewing fun and partly what makes presents interesting.

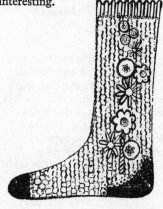

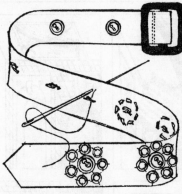

To make this last belt proceed as follows:

1. Collect together as many beads, old metal, bone or pearl buttons as you can find—an assortment of sizes is best—together with various rings, loops and other decorative oddments.

2. Wash these beads, buttons, etc., in mild soapy water, using a soft scrubbing brush to get into the corners and grooves, and dry them thoroughly with

Decorative belts can also be made in many different ways, such as by plaiting ribbons together—as shown below; making the basic belt shape with the aid of a belt kit, available at most notion counters, and then adding decorative beads—as shown on the right; or buying a ready-made webbing belt and covering with a pattern of odd buttons, brass curtain rings, metal loops and other decorative oddments—as shown above.

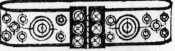

an ordinary hairdryer and soft towel to prevent rust and staining.

3. Arrange them into a pleasing pattern on a cheap webbing or fabric belt, and using silk buttonhole twist stitch each button, bead and loop into position by hand, starting with the largest. These should be sewn on at regular intervals, with the smaller ones being attached in a decorative pattern around them and a few extra novelties scattered in between.

67

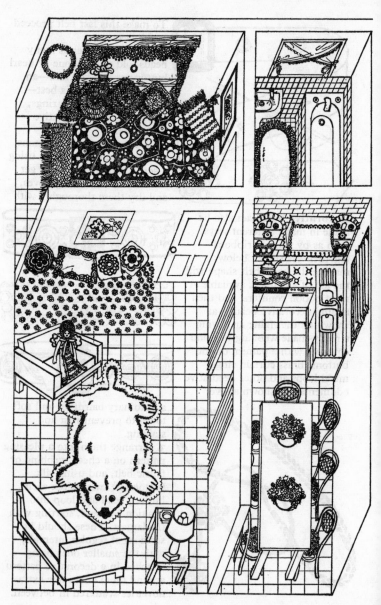

3. Sewing For The House

In this chapter we are going to explain the simplest way of making things for the home. For these, as for the other suggestions throughout this book, we have specially chosen methods which—though slightly unorthodox—are easily understood and produce quick and satisfying results. Making things for your home by using these methods can be the most exciting and personally rewarding type of sewing. However beginners would be well advised to tackle some of the simplest things first before attempting the more complex items, for the excitement of completing and hanging your first simple curtain will be very rewarding whereas if through inexperience you make a bed cover which does not fit, you will only be disappointed.

The following twenty-eight pages are only intended as an introduction to sewing for the house, while the methods of sewing described in the other chapters of this book are intended to be liberally interpreted and will help you develop original ideas of your own. Do remember to avoid the discouraging jargon and complexities of traditional craft techniques. Instead, choose the most straightforward methods, interesting but simple patterns and striking colours, so that your sewing will be quick, easy, and exciting to do.

Finally, always be on the look-out for new ideas: this is partly what makes sewing for the home both interesting and fun. If you are making a bedspread or some new cushions spend a little time looking through those in a big store to see how they are made and decorated. If you are making some curtains or a chair cover, don't just remake them from the same fabric you always use; instead spend a little time browsing through various fabric shops comparing colours, textures, patterns and prices. If you are thinking of making new blinds or a rug look at some recent magazines for ideas. A scrap-book is a most valuable thing to add to your sewing equipment. Collect in it all sorts of designs which you think are successful: photographs of interesting surface treatments, details from articles on furnishing trends, fabric samples, etc. When you are thinking of making something new you will only have to turn to your scrap-book to find a wealth of ideas to help crystallize your thoughts, in much the same way as a book of cooking

recipes helps when planning a meal. You will find that a scrapbook kept up-to-date will become just as important to your needlework as your scissors or pins.

The bathroom. Many things can be made for the bathroom, including colourful chequerboard towels with matching flannel glove, comfortable bath head-rests, matching cushions and seat covers, bathroom tidies, curtains or decorative rugs. Just a few ideas are shown on the following six pages but many more can be designed and made by those who enjoy this kind of sewing.

Decorative towels can be made out of pretty coloured towellings, which you can purchase by the yard at most fabric counters. These towels may be as complex as the beach towel shown on page 104, or plain coloured with a deep string fringe stitched on to each end. A matching hand flannel can also be made by stitching a small rectangle together so that it fits on the hand, rather like a child's mitten, and adding a coloured hanging tape or cord if required.

Head-rest. A simple rectangular head-rest, similar to the one shown opposite, can be made out of a large bathroom flannel.

First seam the two flat sides of a flannel together, the right side inside, and then turn through to form a tube. One inch from one end stitch the tube edges together to form a sucker flange.

Next fill a polythene sandwich bag with foam pieces and seal up the end with Sellotape. Slip this into another polythene bag and then into a third, reversing the open ends each time so that the filling is waterproof. Slip this inner form into the head-rest and close tube by stitching 1″ from end.

Finally, sew on four rubber suckers to the back of the 1″ end flanges.

Bathroom tidy. These can be made in sailcloth, deck-chair canvas or similar firm waterproof fabric. The one illustrated on the right shows how tidies can be made to hold such things as brushes and combs, curlers and hair pins, mirrors and scissors, as well as bathroom slippers. In fact they can be designed and made to any size for any special tidying job that your bathroom needs. Simply cut a rectangle of canvas to the size required and add various pockets and loops as needed. If you are making a children's tidy then add some fun decoration, together with a special secret pocket for their unaccountable treasures and bathroom toys. In this way you will encourage them to use the tidy, and you will find that your bathroom will look neater and more decorative.

Bathroom cushions. Like those explained on pages 77 and

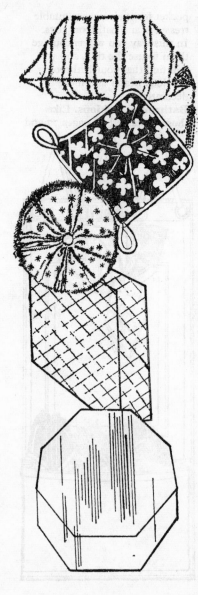

78, or garden cushions explained on pages 99 and 100, bathroom cushions can be made in all sorts of ways and in a great variety of fabrics, but they will obviously be only as practical as the fabric used. These can range from shiny plastic and PVC, to sailcloth or towelling, and made to go with curtains, seat covers, bathtowels or a rug. Preferably the cushion should be made around an inner waterproof shape, which can be bought ready-made at most stores, or the filling can be packed inside several layers of sheet polythene or polythene bags before slotting into the cover. Apart from this there are no other rules, so simply follow the general instructions already given, and those on page 78 etc.

Seat covers can be made to fit over most bathroom chairs, stools, or a w.c. lid. Generally these covers are best made in terry or stretch towelling, although other soft fabrics could also be used.

First cut your fabric shape 2″–3″ larger all round than the object to be covered, then either crease over $\frac{1}{2}$″ and stitch flat, or, if the fabric is too thick, bind in bias strip. Next, fold over 1″ all round and tack flat, easing in any fullness evenly before stitching $\frac{1}{4}$″ from inside edge right round the shape, but leaving a 1″ gap at the back. Slot a length of $\frac{1}{4}$″ or $\frac{1}{2}$″ elastic through this gap with the aid of a bodkin or safety-pin and pass right round inside the turning. Place cover in position and draw out enough elastic to hold the cover there firmly before knotting the elastic ends. To remove for washing simply pull off, unknotting and removing the elastic if necessary.

Bathroom rugs can be made out of a simple rectangle or oval of thick terry towelling backed

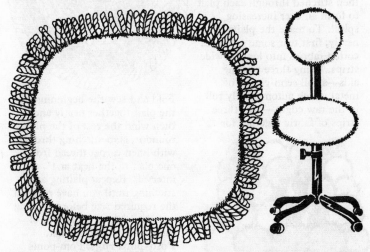

with a sheet of ½" thick underlay polythene foam or latex, and edged in string fringe, as shown below, or they can be made in any of the other following six ways.

Towelling rug. Cut a rectangle or oval of terry towelling the size required and also cut exactly the same shape in ½" thick polythene foam underlay, which can be purchased by the

yard at most large stores. Tack-stitch the towelling and polythene together edge to edge and then bind in wide bias strip. Tack, then hand-stitch, some string fringe around the shape so that the fringe webbing covers up the bound edge.

Fringed rug. These can be made by stitching strips of cheap string fringing on to a soft canvas backing, or they can

be made by using a rug needle and special string loops, which are knotted through a rug-maker's canvas backing. All these items may be purchased at most notion counters in the larger stores or specialist shops.

Rag rugs can be made for both the bedroom and bathroom, as well as for other rooms if required. These rugs are made from small strips of fabric—

½" to 1" wide and 3" to 4" long—which are looped through an open weave canvas with a rug needle and the ends then passed through the loop and pulled tight, in much the same way as the fringed rug explained on the previous page.

Plaited rugs are made from long strands of fabric pieces, 1" wide, which are plaited together three at a time and then stitched through each plait to form an ever increasing spiral. To make the plaits neatly, first tear some colourful cotton fabrics into long 1" wide strips. Using three plaiting aids—small semi-circles of metal which automatically roll in the raw edges—plait three strips of fabric together for 12".

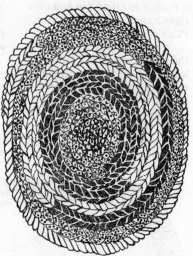

Fold and sew the beginning of the plait together neatly and then wind the rest of the plait round it, stab-stitching through with linen carpet thread from one plait to the next at 1" intervals. Repeat plaiting and stitching until you have reached the required size before sticking and stitching on a backing of canvas and rubber or felt.

Pom-pom rugs. Pom-poms forming a pattern, or simply scattered at random, can be stitched on to a canvas or felt backing. The pom-poms could be made out of rug wool, ribbons, ½" wide strips of cotton fabric, knitting wool or many other materials. To make the pom-poms first cut out two stiff cardboard circles the size of a cocoa-tin lid, making a ½"–¾" hole in the centre of each. Place

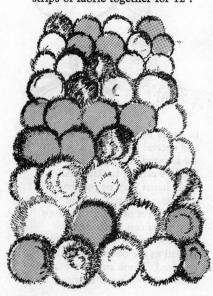

fabric rugs. Simply knit or crochet the shape required, or join many small samples together to form an interesting patchwork. Mount these on to a felt backing, random stab-stitching at 2″–3″ intervals to hold the two layers together. Mark on the finished shape required and machine stitch together around these marks. Cut shape and then bind edge with bias strip, as shown below. **Furry rugs.** A simple rectangular rug can be made from fur fabric and trimmed with a contrasting fringe, as shown on the left, or you could cut the fur fabric into an

both cards together and cover them completely by slotting through and wrapping round the rug wool or ribbons. When the whole circumference of the card is covered slip the scissor points between the two card circles and cut all the threads at the outside edge. Next, draw a 9″ length of twine between the two circles, winding it tightly around the centre threads several times and then fasten it off with a knot. Leave the ends long enough to thread through the backing. Remove cards and repeat.

Knitted rugs or rugs made of crochet can be made and used in much the same way as most

animal shape as shown below.

To make this type of bear-skin rug you must first cut a brown paper pattern to the size and shape required, experimenting with several patterns before cutting into the fur fabric.

Having cut the exact paper pattern the next thing is to pencil this shape on to the plain back of the fur fabric and then

them together around the body shape. Cut two ear shapes and a tail and sew these into position before trimming off the excess felt with pinking shears, or scalloping the edge as required.

Finally sew on a dark nose patch, two beaded eyes and looped rug-wool claws.

Children's things. Many functional as well as decorative

cut it out, using just the tips of the scissors to avoid cutting the pile. An alternative method is to cut out with a metal-backed razor blade, again using just the point.

Next, make a small oval head pad, which should be about 3″ deep and 2″ smaller all round than the head. Place the bear-shaped fur fabric and oval head pad on to a large rectangle of coloured felt and hand-stitch

things can easily be made for children's rooms; particularly toys, fun cushions, bedding and bed covers, curtains, wall-hangings, hot-water bottle covers and pyjama cases, etc. Some of these are explained on the following six pages, while many more are explained in other chapters of this book. The basic methods for sewing all these items are in fact the same as those described

throughout this book, so if a particular decorative technique or interesting stitch appeals to you simply adapt our suggestions to fit your own ideas. Our aim is to help you make your nursery things more interesting and exciting, both to look at and to make.

Nursery cushions, follow much the same making and designing techniques as those used for animal and toy cushions, explained on pages 13 and 14, and for normal cushions explained on the following two pages. However do avoid using any easily detachable trimmings as these could be a potential danger to very young children. Generally speaking it is better to concentrate on large bold areas in striking colour combinations rather than intricately sewn details.

Another possibility, instead of filling the toy shape with kapok, is to sew an 8" zip fastener on to the turning-through gap so that it can be used for a nightie case, as explained on page 25.

Making cushions. There are about as many different ways of making these as there are people sewing, for cushions can be all sorts of shapes and sizes, covered in all sorts of fabrics, decorated with all kinds of different surface treatments, and made with various technical methods. The only guiding principle is if the cushion looks right and is either useful or decorative; then it is a good cushion. Whereas a beautifully

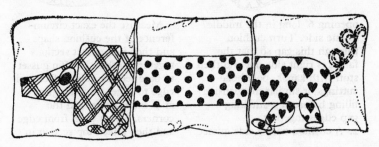

sewn but ugly or uncomfortable cushion is far better forgotten by making another to take its place.

1. To make a simple cushion cut two identical squares of fabric and lay them together face to face with edges exactly matching. Stitch all round ½″ in, leaving a turning-through

is best made to fit an existing inner cushion, a polythene foam or latex shape. Cut two rectangular sections of fabric ½″ larger all round than the inner shape. Now cut a gusset section 1″ wider than the depth required, and long enough to go right round, plus extra for side seam allowance.

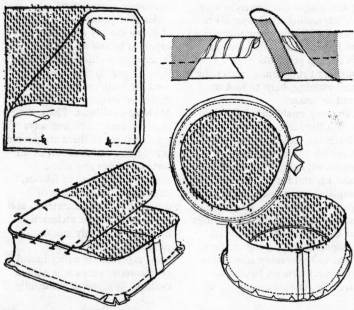

opening 6″ long in the middle of one side. Turn cushion through this gap so that the fabric is right side out and then stuff with kapok, polythene cuttings or similar inexpensive filling before slip-stitching gap edges together.

2. A cushion with a side gusset

Measure the exact circumference of the cushion shape and then join gusset sections together to this size. Pin gusset to base section, face to face and edge to edge, snipping gusset at ½″ intervals around the corners. Stitch ½″ in from edge and then attach top section in the same way, but leaving one end open for inserting the inner shape before finally slip-stitching gap together.

3. Piped cushions are made in exactly the same way as ordinary cushions except a specially made piping section is introduced in between the fabric pieces being joined

Using a piping foot machine stitch close to the cord, join any odd lengths together as shown on the page opposite, top right.

4. To apply the piping, simply pin, tack and then machine the piping into position, with raw edges of piping matching raw edges of fabric, lapping the join as shown on the left. Complete

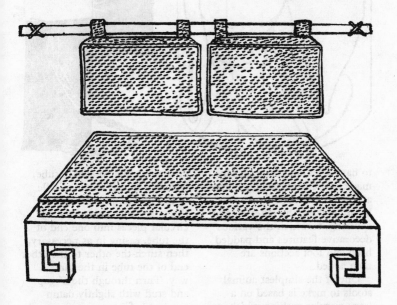

together.

First cut several lengths of 1″ wide crossway fabric strips and join these together to form a continuous strip. Fold this strip around a piping cord so that the raw edges meet, then tack stitch through the turnings so that the cord is pushed tightly against the folded edge.

the cushion in the normal way.

Animal stools. Many delightful animal stools, interestingly decorated and specially shaped, can be made by following the general instructions set out for animal-shaped cushions on page 13, the only real difference apart from their size, being that it is better for these stools

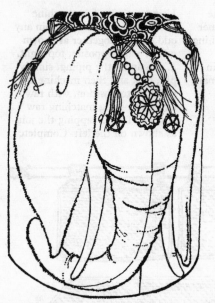

to have an inner cushion shape
made out of heavyweight calico
and stuffed with damp sawdust
before making the outer animal
covering, to which the various
decorative features and padded
head and foot sections are
then added.

One of the simplest animal
stools to make is based on a
large circular cushion which can
then be formed into an elephant,
frog, broody chicken, tortoise,
hedgehog, or even a large
mouse.

1. Cut two 13″ circles of
heavyweight calico, using a
large dinner plate as a guide,
and cut a 40″ × 12″ strip for the
side gusset.

Stitch the 12″ edges of the

gusset together to form a tube,
leaving a 6″ gap in the middle
of the stitching for turning
through. Stitch one of the 13″
circular pieces into one end of
the tube, easing in as necessary,
then stitch the other to the other
end of the tube in the same
way. Turn through the 6″ gap
and stuff with slightly damp
sawdust before sewing gap
edges together.

2. To make the cover cut one
circle of plain or patterned
furnishing fabric slightly larger
than the original calico ones,
13½″–14″ wide, and two gusset
strips 22″ long by 15″ wide.
Join the gusset side seams by
laying the two rectangular
pieces together face to face and

stitching down both 15″ side seams. Next stitch the 13½″ circle into one end, again with fabrics face to face.

Turn fabric pieces to right side and slip over the top of the sawdust-filled shape. If the outer cover is a little loose add a layer of cheap wadding around the inner shape; if it is too tight simply remove some of the sawdust. If you want a curved top add extra wadding to obtain the shape required.

3. Using some brightly-coloured pieces of felt or contrasting fabric cut two pairs of ear shapes, which should be stitched together and stuffed with kapok. Next cut out an interesting head shape and again stuff with kapok. Remove the cover and stick and stitch the ears and head into position, adding other extra sections as required. Slip the cover on again.

4. Using a curved carpet needle and linen carpet thread sew the bottom turnings on to the bottom of the sawdust-filled shape. Now cut a 12″ circular piece of felt and stick, then stitch, this on to the base to cover any raw edges.

Finally, add beaded eyes, braiding, coloured stick-ons and any other decorative extras you like as explained for the many other things in this book.

Lampshades. Most lampshades are very simple to cover, requiring no more than an evening's work, and no special tools—just normal things like sharp scissors, dressmakers' chalk, needles and pins, a little UHU glue, sufficient fabric for covering, and some matching tape or bias binding.

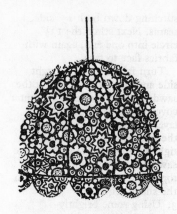

1. Cut tape for covering the side spokes 1½ times the length of each and bind from top to bottom, slot-knotting neatly at

and then pin the fabric to the taped top and bottom rings, again pulling tight. Mark round all the lines of pins with dressmakers' chalk. Take out the pins and then cut the shape, leaving ½" turning allowance all round.

the base as shown above. Cut a piece of tape to twice top ring length and bind as for spokes, binding the bottom ring in a similar way and enclosing all the tape ends.

2. Next cut a rectangle of fabric on the crossway grain large enough to cover either a quarter or half of the frame, allowing an extra 2" all round. Pin fabric to frame and pull firmly to shape along each side

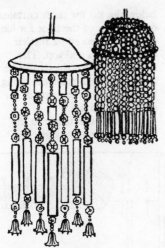

lines are running evenly with the spokes. Turn in the top and bottom raw edges and sew these firmly and neatly to the frame, pinning out as necessary.

4. Add any braid or fringing, sticking with UHU glue or Copydex before neatly sewing.

Other easy-to-make lampshades include those covered in raffia or ribbons, paper or parchment, beads or crochet. Yet others can be decorated with various stick-ons of coloured

3. Cut remaining sections using the pin-marked shape as a guide, and then stitch together using a simple, flat open or self-neatening French seam. Place cover over the frame, pulling and pinning firmly into position, and making sure that the seam

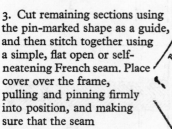

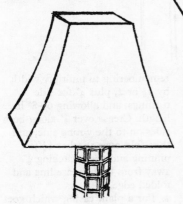

pieces of plastic, sequins and felt shapes, dried flowers, lace motifs, embroidered cordings, appliqués, bobble edgings, coloured fringings, tassels—or indeed anything which looks both interesting and decorative, as explained for the many other items shown throughout this and our previous book.

So try your skill at decorating, as well as making, your next lampshade.

83

Simple curtains can be made in a great variety of fabrics, ranging from plain terylene net to intricately patterned silk brocades, with lots of pretty printed cotton fabrics in between; while the styles range from the straight up-and-down to festoons and swags enriched with pleats and pelmets, fringes and tassels,

below the sill for short curtains, or just clear of the floor for long ones, and then add a further 6″–8″ for hem and top. The width of the curtain should be at least 1½ or 2 times the fixing width, allowing an extra 2″ for each side turning.

1. Cut out your fabric to the width and length required,

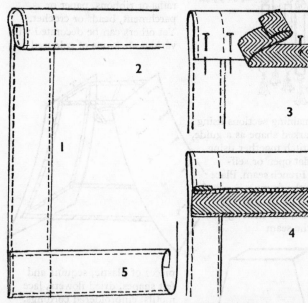

with decorative tie-backs and matching blinds.

Unlined curtains. The first thing to do is measure your windows correctly. Measure the top length of the fixing rod or track, which should extend 2″–3″ beyond the window on each side. Next measure the depth from the fixing rod to just

remembering to multiply width by 1½ or 2, plus 4″ for side turnings, and allowing 6″–8″ in length. Crease over ½″ along both sides on to the wrong side, and then fold over another 1½″, pinning and then stitching ⅛″ away from both crease line and folded edge.

2. For a plain casing which goes

over a rod or wire, crease over and stitch the top as for the side turnings.

3. For a track fixing, cut a length of Rufflette tape 4″ longer than the curtain width, knotting cord ends together on under side of tape 2″ from each end. Fold curtain material over $1\frac{1}{2}″$ at top and pin flat, covering the raw edges with the Rufflette tape and then stitching $\frac{1}{8}″$ from each edge and tucking in the 2″ side seam allowance.

4. Pull out both cords until curtain is the correct width, distributing fullness evenly. Do not cut off the surplus cord; instead wind it round a piece of card which can be safety-pinned out of sight. Slot in hooks at regular 2″–3″ intervals.

5. Slip the curtain into position and mark the exact length required. Crease in $\frac{1}{2}″$ from the bottom raw edge and then pin and stitch hem to exact length $\frac{1}{4}″$ below crease, and again $\frac{1}{4}″$ from folded edge as shown on the left. If you wish to allow for possible shrinkage, add an extra 1″ for every 3 ft. of curtain length. Use this extra length for a deeper hem which should be unpicked and let down before laundering.

Decorative tablecloth. If you want to make some new table linen many of the decorative techniques explained in this book can be used to great advantage; particularly for casual at-home, informal entertaining,

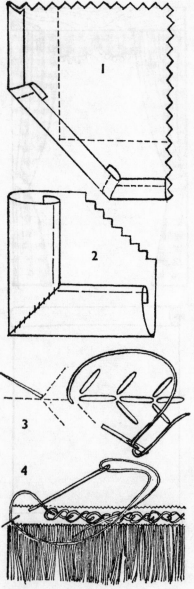

outdoor picnics or party evenings, but also for formal dinners.

As with all other kinds of sewing, first spend a little time looking around the shops and stores, magazines and news-papers, and also thumb through this book, turning to pages 51, 89, 92 and 93, etc., for ideas on all sorts of decoration. Bold embroidery can be used, or appliqué, coloured cut-outs, open threadwork and all sorts of decorative edgings. We would emphasise the importance of not getting bogged-down with the usual mumbo-jumbo of traditional sewing methods, for needlework certainly need not be such a laborious chore as the traditionalists make it sound. Instead, be as creative as you can by using simple patterns, interesting but not necessarily intricate designs and striking colours, and sewing methods which are easy and straight-forward. Your sewing will then be exciting and fun to do.

1. Buy a piece of even weave fabric the length required—generally 2–3 yards of 54″ wide fabric is sufficient. Trim away selvedge $\frac{1}{2}$″ in from both edges and then trim across both ends exactly on the grain. Crease over $\frac{1}{4}$″ to wrong side all round and machine stitch to hold flat.

Next fold and press the hem 1″ in all round. At corners fold inwards diagonally on to the 1″ crease line and then cut away the corner, leaving ¼″ seam allowance.

2. Refold the hem, tacking up into position and then slip-stitching the diagonal mitre together. Stitch hem into position by using a normal dressmakers' hemming slip stitch, or by machining ⅛″ from both the creased and folded

other stitches shown on pages 51 or 95, etc.

4. If you want to add a string fringe then simply attach by first pinning it accurately into position and then either slip-stitching it, or embroidering it on with a chain stitch or twisted chain, as shown opposite.

5. Finally make some matching

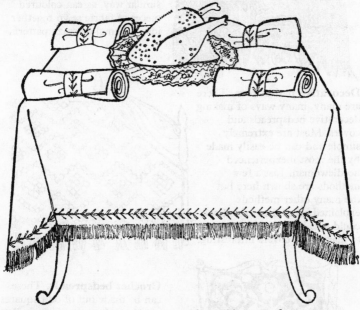

edges, or by using a decorative embroidery stitch.

3. If you would like an embroidered hem finish, use the simple fern stitch shown on the left. This is simply three straight stitches of equal length radiating from the same point, as shown, diagram 3. You could also use one of the

table napkins out of an extra length of fabric—six being made out of 1 yard of 54″ fabric if they are cut into equal 18″ squares—stitching and decorating them in the same way as the tablecloth. See also pages 102 and 103 for other ideas for out-of-doors picnic and garden party table linen.

Knitted patchwork bed covers, similar to the one shown on the left, can be made out of a number of 8″ or 9″ squares, worked in brightly-coloured wools and different stitches. Simply sew the knitted squares together forming a completely random pattern. Crochet squares can also be used in a similar way, as can coloured pieces of fabric sewn together into a formal or crazy pattern.

Decorative bed covers. There are many, many ways of making decorative bedspreads and covers. Most are extremely simple and can be easily made by the most inexperienced needlewoman. Just a few methods are shown here but the many other methods explained throughout this book could also be easily adapted to make your covers interesting.

Crochet bedspreads. These can be made out of odd squares of coloured crochet in a similar way to knitted patchwork bed covers previously explained, or they can be crocheted into a more formal pattern as illustrated above. An introduction to simple crochet is given on the following two pages which explains how easy this lacey fabric is to make.

Braid Embroidery as shown on the right and on page 92, is made by stitching coloured braids and cords into an interesting pattern. The areas which are left between the braids can be filled with appliqués of coloured fabric and various embroidery stitches. A detachable bed-head cover can also be made using the same braid embroidery.

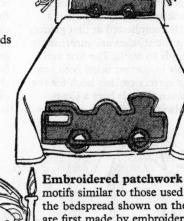

Embroidered patchwork motifs similar to those used on the bedspread shown on the left, are first made by embroidering separate pieces of coloured fabrics which are then trimmed to shape before being pinned into position. The flowers are then stitched where required, and embroidered stems and leaves added using the stitches shown on pages 51, 92 and 95, etc.

Coloured appliqué. The bedspread shown on the right has a cut edge appliqué of coloured felts, stuck and stitched into position and then enriched with various embroidery stitches, couching and braidwork, as explained for felt wall-hangings on pages 94 and 95. Traditional turned-edge fabric patchworked appliqué can also be used in a similar way.

89

Simple crochet. This interesting method of making lacey fabric by the simple use of hook and thread may seem a little complicated at first glance, but the stitches are surprisingly simple to work. The first and most important thing is to buy the correct crochet hook for the chosen thread; here a Coats/Milward needlework stockist will

1. Loop the thread round the little finger of the left hand, across the palm and behind the forefinger, pulling the loop closed around the crochet hook.
2. Pass the hook under thread and catch the thread with the hook—'threading over'. Draw thread through the loop on hook making one chain stitch (ch.st.). Repeat step 3 until you have as

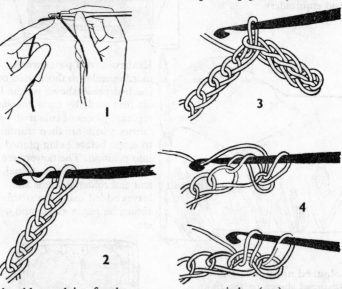

be able to advise, for the threads can vary from the readily obtainable Mercer-Crochet threads, available in a very beautiful colour range, to dyed string, braids, raffia, ribbons, coloured wools, etc.

Chain stitch (ch.st.). Make a simple loop at the end of the thread through which the crochet needle can be passed.

many stitches (sts.) as you need, remembering that one loop must always remain on the hook and that your left thumb and forefinger should be kept near to the stitch on which you are working.

3. **Slip stitch** (s.st.). Having made between 20 and 30 ch.sts. work back along the chain with slip stitches (s.sts.) by inserting

the hook from the front under the two top threads of each ch.st. to the left of hook, catching thread with hook—'threading over'—and drawing through, keeping the new loop on hook. Repeat with next ch.st., etc.

4. **Double crochet** (d.c.). Insert hook from the front under the two top threads of second ch.st. from hook, catch thread and draw thread through so that you have two loops on hook. Thread over and draw through two loops so that only one loop is left on hook, making one double crochet stitch (dc.st.) as diagram 5.

6. **Treble crochet** (tr.) is similar to double crochet but is worked with three loops on the hook instead of two. Pass hook under the thread of left hand, insert hook into stitch, thread over and pull through so that three loops are on hook, thread over and pull through two loops on hook as in diagram 7. Thread over again and pull through remaining two loops, one loop now remains as diagram 8.

The stitches illustrated are only a few of the numerous kinds which can be used in crochet. Many more basic and decorative stitches can easily be learnt from the easy-to-follow crochet pamphlets published by the *Coats Sewing Group*, and available through most Mercer-Crochet needlework

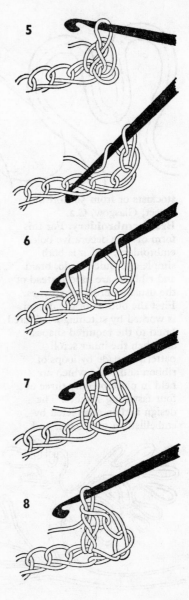

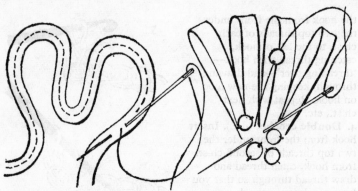

stockists or from 50 Bothwell Street, Glasgow, C.2.

Braid embroidery. For this form of very decorative bold embroidery, which is both simple and quick to do, braid and ribbons are used instead of the usual embroidery stitches. First the outline of the design is worked by stitching a coloured braid to the required shapes and then the inner scroll pattern is made by loops of ribbon and braid which are held in place by only three or four fastening stitches. The design is then completed by embellishing with beads and various embroidery stitches.

Outline braiding, as shown below, is made by sewing down various coloured braids around the outlines of the traced pattern or transfer design. The stitches are usually small back stitches $\frac{1}{8}''$ long and worked every $\frac{3}{8}''$ in the centre of the braid, although a simple running stitch or machine stitch is equally effective. At the curves of the pattern ease the braid smoothly around the outside edge so that the inside is slightly full. The curves can then be pressed to shrink the braid into shape.

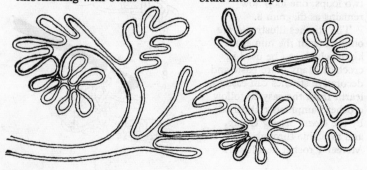

Braid flowers, as shown below, are made by looping lengths of coloured braid and ribbons into a pleasing pattern, and then securing each loop with several hand stitches at both top and bottom. The looped 'flowers' are then decorated with beads and embroidery stitches as illustrated on the top right-section, with additional couching and embroidery stitches being added as desired.

Various coloured shapes of felt and fabric can also be used in conjunction with braid embroidery. These shapes should first of all be roughly edge stitched into place and then the raw edges covered and

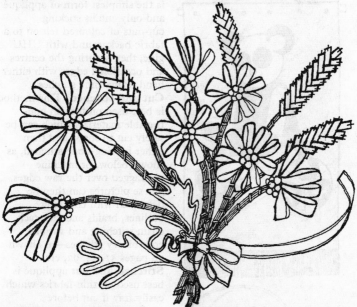

hand corner of the opposite page. The ears of corn are even more quickly made, and a single stitch on the top fold forms the beard, whilst a smaller stitch is used at the juncture of the ends. The whole design is then completed by stitching lengths of cord or braid between each looped permanently fixed by outlining in braid, cord and couching before adding bead and embroidery embellishments.

Appliqué. This form of surface decoration is made by sticking and stitching various cut-out pieces of differently coloured fabrics on to a contrasting background, and then enriching

93

and unifying the design with embroidery, braiding and linking stitches. Success depends as much on the neatness of stitching as it does on the boldness of the design, as well as the complementing or contrasting use of both colour and textures.

Stuck and stitched appliqué is the simplest form of appliqué and only entails sticking cut-outs of coloured felt on to a fabric background with UHU glue, then securing the centres and occasional edges with either hand or machine stitches.

Cut and stitched. This method is best used on firmish non-frayable materials which can be safely cut to shape and then either herring-bone stitched, as shown below, or machine zig-zagged over the raw edges. These pictures can then be decorated with couching outlines, braids and rick rack, chain stitching and various embroidery stitches—as shown on pages 51, 54, 92, etc.

Stitched and cut appliqué is best used on thin fabrics which easily fray if cut before appliquing. Simply cut a larger area of fabric than is needed, marking on the exact shape required, which is then zig-zag stitched through on to the main fabric before trimming off the surplus fabric edges.

Turned edge. The turned-in method of appliqué is used as an alternative to the stitched and cut method for thin frayable fabrics. First cut a template of stiff paper the exact size and shape required— pages from a glossy monthly magazine or card from a cereal packet are ideal—then cut a piece of fabric ¼″–¾″ larger than the template. Next turn in the edges over the card and crease them flat with a warm iron, tacking any difficult edges to hold accurately. After pressing the turnings flat remove the paper template and any tacking, then slip-stitch into position, or use side stitch as shown above right, or blanket stitch as shown below. Finally, boldly decorate with areas of embroidery stitches, beads, couching and braidwork, etc., as shown on various other pages in this and our companion books.

Patchwork can also be successfully combined with appliqué work. Simply join several coloured shapes of cotton or similar fabrics together in the traditional patchwork method, using triangular, rectangular or diamond shaped pieces which have been turned-in over templates as explained for turned-edge appliqué. These formal shapes are then slip stitched together before being incorporated into the appliqué work.

Patchwork pictures or wall-hangings can be made in many ways, from the simple felt stuck-and-stitched nursery

pictures shown on pages 94 and 95, to the intricately worked family portrait shown opposite—done in a mixture of coloured and textured fabrics and embellished with embroidery stitches, braids and beads, raffia, coloured wools and strands of leather and plastic.

As explained earlier, the choice of design is unlimited as there are no hard and fast rules governing the sewing techniques. If you enjoy experimenting you can make a patchwork picture in any way, and by any method, you choose. The only criterion is whether you, your family and friends like the finished picture, and if it looks right hanging in the room for which it was designed.

Before you start making a patchwork picture spend a little time looking through some nicely illustrated books. If you are making a nursery picture look through Kate Greenaway's illustrations for Mother Goose, one of Dick Bruna's Christmas books, or some of Gallery Five's gift cards. If you wish to make something more sophisticated then look at one of Edmund Dulac's picture books; or if you would like to make an 'op-pop' art or space-age-inspired picture you could work from a Dr Who's weekly. Having looked at these various illustrations, try putting different pleasing shapes and interesting textures together to get a feel of the design, shifting the cut-outs around to obtain the best design balance before sewing them into place. These pictures should be your own personal creations, and not simply sewn copies of other people's artworks, for it is the personal touch and variation on an idea which makes a patchwork picture interesting, rather than the less imaginative and laboured copying line-for-line of a Rubens or Van Gogh.

Try experimenting with different techniques, combining braid embroidery—explained on pages 92 and 93—with stuck and stitched appliqué work from page 95, or embroidery stitches from page 51 with some beading from page 54 and felt decoration from page 14. Start by roughing out your design with coloured felt-tipped pens, as explained on page 121, and try making your own fringed hem as shown on page 125; in fact try anything which encourages you to sew. But remember that whatever your final choice, your patchwork picture must be interesting to look at, and have bold colours and exciting textures, and that all these things should have been used with the maximum of ease and pleasure and the minimum of skill and trouble. For a picture which is beautifully sewn but dull in design or over-laboured is far better forgotten by making another to take its place.

4. Sewing for Out-of-Doors

Sewing for out-of-doors, whether it is for the garden, the beach, or for the country, is a very exciting and rewarding type of sewing, for it is here that so many decorative and useful things can be made without having to compromise too much with the established surroundings. When sewing for out-of-doors you can try out that extra bold decorative detailing or unusual colouring which, in a

room, might be too dominating but which will look fine in the open. You can use a pretty coloured cotton print for some garden seats; or some striped towelling with a deep cotton fringe for a beach towel, with matching bikini, beach-bag and cushion; you could make a play tent out of the same material used for a kite; or plan a decorative garden swing made in the same way as a hammock.

The following twenty-nine pages are only intended as an introduction to sewing for out-of-doors, while the general methods of sewing in the other chapters of this book—and our previous book *Streamlined Curtains and Covers*—are intended to be liberally interpreted.

As with all other kinds of sewing, first spend a little time looking around the shops and stores, in magazines and newspapers, collecting as many notes and press cuttings as possible so that these can be used in much the same way as cooking recipes. However, do remember to avoid getting involved in the off-putting

explained on pages 78 and 79. However, certain types of fabric are obviously more suited to outdoor use, such as deckchair canvas, sailcloth, bold patch-worked linens or plastic coated fabrics. Remember that the cushion will only be as practical as the fabric used.

Garden bolster. The long tubular bolster-type cushion

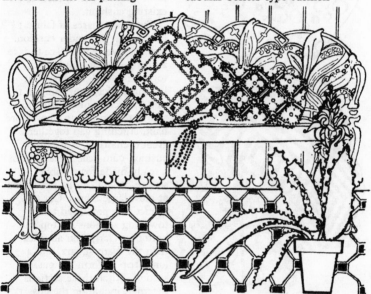

technicalities of traditional needlework. Instead, opt for the simplest methods, simple but interesting patterns, gay colours and designs, so that your sewing will be easy and quick to do.

Outdoor cushions. Garden, picnic or beach cushions follow much the same principles of construction as those already

shown overleaf is made from 1 yard of striped deckchair canvas, with small pieces of foam rubber as a filling.

First cut a strip 27" wide right across the width of canvas, then seam the two raw edges together from selvedge to selvedge, leaving a 6" gap in the middle. Next cut two 9"

filling with polythene foam pieces, before hand-stitching the centre gap together.

Waterproof cushions. The second cushion on the left is a simple square made from $\frac{1}{2}$ yard of bobble-finished plasticized cotton. For this cushion it is best to cover an under shape of polythene or latex in calico, or to recover an existing cushion.

Cut two squares of fabric $1\frac{1}{2}''$ larger than the under cushion. Lay the two fabrics face to face and edge to edge and stitch together round all sides, but leaving sufficient opening in the middle section of one side to slot in the under cushion before hand-stitching gap together.

Beach cushion. A useful cushion-cum-seat is made from a ready-made foam rubber square, which can be purchased at most large stores. Cut two attractively patterned terry towelling sections for top and bottom, $1''$ larger on all sides than the foam square, and a long strip to form the gusset section. Stitch these sections together, including the gusset, $\frac{1}{2}''$ from edges all round, but leaving one edge completely open for turning through and for slotting in the inner foam shape before stitching gap together. Alternatively a zip fastener can be inserted along one edge to allow for easy removal for washing.

Embroidered cushions. All

circles out of the remaining fabric, using an ordinary plate as a cutting guide, and stitch one circle on to each end of the tube, taking approximately $\frac{1}{2}''$ turnings and easing slightly to fit evenly into position.

Now turn the bolster cushion cover through the centre gap

sorts of simple embroidery stitches can be made with most automatic sewing machines, while many more stitches and traditional motifs can be hand-worked as explained on pages 51, 93 and 95. Among the numerous materials which can be used are string, raffia, braids, leather, plastic, beads, dried seeds, ribbons and many more novelties. Just look around and buy the best and most interesting for your cushion design.

Appliqué patterns, together with formal, random or crazy patchwork make very decorative cushions for garden use, especially if made with bold carrying loops—as shown below—or teamed to make interesting sets—as can be seen on the right. Simply follow the basic techniques already explained in this book, adding various cut-outs with UHU glue and strengthening with a few bold stitches as on page 89 etc.

Picnic set. With the increasingly popular vogue for eating out-of-doors, in the garden, on

a patio, having a barbecue or a picnic, some new ideas for table linen have also become fashionable. Needless to say, these ideas could also be adapted for informal 'at-home' use.

When planning your table linen for this kind of informal entertaining remember that novelty is no less important than neat sewing. Part of the fun is adapting ideas you have seen in magazines, newspapers, shops or even television programmes, so that what you make is really your own creation. Just a few basic ideas are given here.

Open threadwork. Traditional drawn threadwork, Hardanger or Richelieu work, makes simple plain-woven linens look strikingly attractive, particularly if very bright colours are used and mixed with the more traditional ones: burnt orange or lettuce green, for example, mixed with natural pale biscuit or scarlet and navy used together.

Bold embroidery. Big, abstract flower embroidery on plain coloured linens finished with a deep cotton fringe—which can be either white or dyed—is another way of dressing a table decoratively. There are many transfer designs on sale at most embroidery counters, but for this you should choose a very simple formalized one which relies on its bold colouring and distinctive shape for effect.

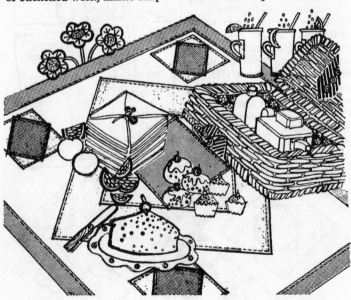

There are also many types of embroidery stitches, and here again it is best to choose those which can be quickly and neatly worked rather than the more intricate ones which most of the traditionalists use.

Bold appliqué. This is another idea for decorative table linen, which relies on the bold use of pieces of contrastingly coloured and differently patterned fabrics formed into a pleasing design and teamed with an assortment of patterned and coloured napkins.

Using a plain-colour sailcloth or linen as the main fabric, cut out and stitch on pieces of differently patterned cottons, varying in size and shape, and loop twin pieces of cord over and under so that the whole effect looks like a kite tail—in fact a cut-out kite could be appliquéd on at one end.

Table napkins 18″ square, with a simple rolled-in and stitched edge, are then made to match the various coloured streamers, with napkin rings being made out of the plain coloured sailcloth or linen.

The designs illustrated are only two of many that can be made in this way. The basic methods of construction used are much the same as explained on pages 86 and 87 for a simple tablecloth, with the decoration being applied as required. So try your own skill at designing something different, just for the fun of it.

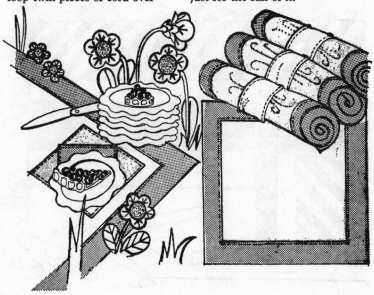

Beach things. Many things can be made for the beach, including strikingly-coloured beach towels with matching cushions—as shown below—a comfortable beach mattress with soft plastic filling and waterproof back and teamed with a matching bikini—as shown opposite—decorative beach-bags as explained on page 106, children's beachwear as shown on pages 109 to 113, or toys and games such as the few shown on pages 114 and 118. But many other things we have illustrated or which you have seen in newspapers, magazines, shops and stores can easily be made simply by following the basic principles explained throughout this book.

Beach towels and cushion sets can be made out of plain and patterned terry towelling purchased by the yard in your local fabric shop. Generally it is best to buy two or three 2-yard lengths; one plain, one striped and one to contrast. Some bold string fringing and matching thread will also be required.

1. To make a pair of beach towels with matching cushions, buy three 2-yard lengths of differing towellings, 6 yards of 3″ string fringing, matching sewing threads and two air cushions, polythene foam or latex cushion shapes.

2. First cut a long strip from the plain towelling 24″ wide, using the full length of the fabric and incorporating the neat selvedge edge. Next cut another long strip from the contrasting towelling 8″ wide, again incorporating the ready-neatened selvedge edge. Finally cut one long strip 16″ wide from the striped towelling.

3. Allowing 1″ for seaming, join the 24″ strip raw edge to the 8″ strip selvedge edge, and then the 8″ strip raw edge to the 16″ strip raw edge. Press these seams open and then stitch each turning flat on to the main section $\frac{1}{2}$″ from seam line. On most towelling this is sufficient neatening, although the spare turning could be clipped to $\frac{1}{8}$″ and cross-stitched down.

4. Turn in $\frac{1}{2}$″ at each end and stitch flat. Finally cover the raw edge with the fringe rib and stitch into place at each end.

5. Cut three more sections in the same way, but using the contrast towelling in place of the plain one, and vice versa etc., for the second towel.

6. Seam the three remaining strips of towelling together and use them to cover either a blow-up cushion or a plastic shape, as explained on page 78.

Beach bed. A simple beach mattress like the one on the left can be made from $2\frac{1}{2}$ yards of towelling, $2\frac{1}{2}$ yards of waterproof canvas or plastic, and $2\frac{1}{4}$ yards of $1\frac{1}{2}$″ thick polythene foam or a blow-up beach mattress.

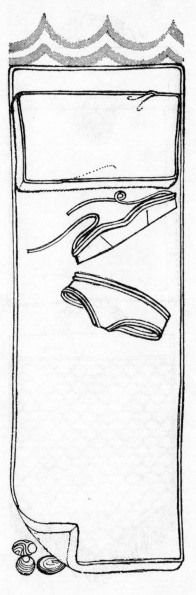

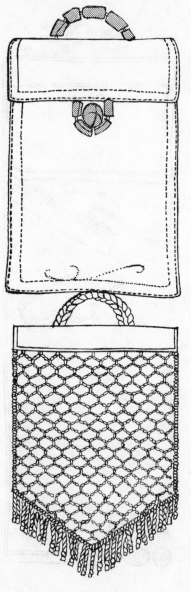

Make the cover in exactly the same way as explained for making a large cushion and then make a matching cushion and a bikini to complete the set.

Beach bags. Many different types of beach bags, picnic or casual bags can easily be made out of all sorts of different materials, and decorated in all sorts of different ways with a variety of trimmings The basic method of construction, however, is simple enough: the material is just stitched inside out and turned through.

Flapped bag. To make the flapped bag on the left cut out a rectangle of sailcloth $1\frac{1}{2}''$ larger than the finished size required, say $14'' \times 10''$. Cut another rectangle $4''$ longer, in this case $18'' \times 10''$.

Turn in first $\frac{1}{4}''$ and then another $\frac{1}{2}''$ on one end of the $14'' \times 10''$ rectangle and double edge stitch flat, so size is now $13\frac{1}{4}'' \times 10''$. Lay the three remaining raw edges on to the corresponding edges of the $18'' \times 10''$ fabric, face to face, and stitch $\frac{3}{4}''$ from the edge right round, fastening off the ends securely. Turn through top opening so right side is outside.

To neaten remaining raw edges, first turn in $\frac{1}{4}''$ and then another $\frac{1}{2}''$ and double edge stitch flat. Now very neatly edge stitch $\frac{1}{8}''$ in all round to hold flat, and again $\frac{3}{8}''$, as shown top left. Finally make a bamboo beaded handle and fastening toggle, using some strong string.

Duffle bag or hold-alls similar to the one shown on the right can be made out of $\frac{1}{2}$ yard of striped canvas or sailcloth together with $2\frac{1}{2}$ yards of coloured webbing and 2 yards of chunky cord.

Cut a rectangle 18″ deep by 27″ wide, and a 9″ circular end section. Stitch the two 18″ edges together, right sides facing, and then stitch in the end section, taking approx. $\frac{1}{2}$″ turnings and easing on slightly as needed. Next turn through top opening so that bag is right side out and then cut an 8″ circle of stiff cardboard and stick with UHU glue inside base turnings.

Cut two 27″ lengths of coloured webbing and seam the ends together to make two 26″ rings. Place one ring over the other, wrong sides facing, and stitch them together $\frac{1}{8}$″ from the top edge. Slot the unstitched side over bag raw edges and stitch through all three thicknesses $\frac{1}{4}$″ from bottom and then $\frac{1}{2}$″ from top and bottom so that they enclose the canvas edge.

Finally, make eight worked eyelets or buy and fix large metal ones at regular intervals around the top—about every $3\frac{1}{4}$″—or ask your local shoe repairer to fix them for you—before slotting in the chunky cord to form the fastening and carrying handles.

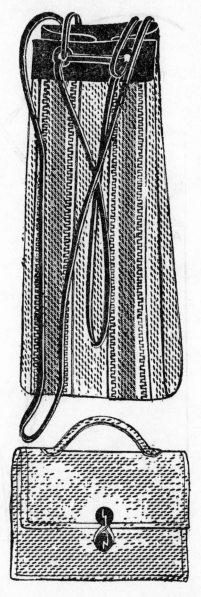

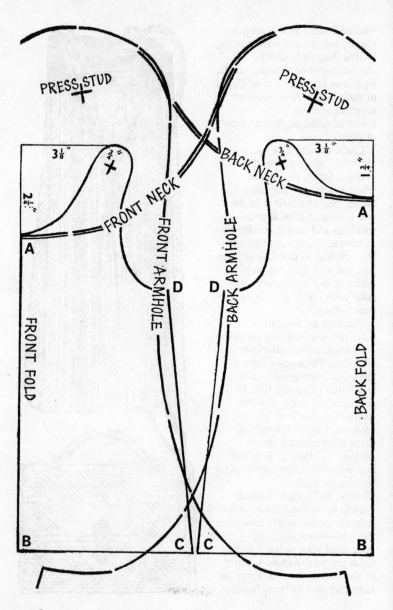

PRESS STUD

PRESS STUD

$3\frac{1}{8}''$

$3\frac{1}{8}''$

$\frac{3}{4}''$

$\frac{3}{4}''$

$1\frac{3}{4}''$

$2\frac{1}{4}''$

A

A

A

BACK NECK

FRONT NECK

FRONT NECK

FRONT ARMHOLE

BACK ARMHOLE

D

D

FRONT FOLD

BACK FOLD

B

C

C

B

Child's beach tunic. To make a simple pattern for a young child's beach tunic you will require a largish sheet of plain wrapping paper, a sheet of tracing or greaseproof paper, a sharp pencil and a ruler.

1. Working from the top left corner of the paper, measure down $2\frac{1}{4}''$ and mark spot A. Continue measuring for length required—plus $2''$ for allowances —i.e., $20''$ for an $18''$ finished length—and mark spot B. From here measure $8\frac{1}{2}''$ across the paper for spot C.

2. Measure $2\frac{1}{2}''$ down from A and then straight across the paper $6\frac{1}{2}''$ for spot D. Draw lines connecting A to B, B to C, and C to D. Next measure across top of paper $3\frac{1}{8}''$ and then down $\frac{3}{4}''$ marking X for press stud position.

3. Using tracing or greaseproof paper mark out front neck shown on the left by the double dashed line, and copy on to your pattern; similarly for the front armhole. Mark A to B 'FRONT FOLD' as shown.

4. Working from top right corner of the paper measure down $1\frac{3}{4}''$ and mark point A. Continue measuring to point B as for the front pattern, and straight across paper $8\frac{1}{2}''$ for point C.

5. Measure down from point A $4''$ and then across paper $6\frac{1}{2}''$ for point D. Draw straight pencil lines connecting A to B, B to C, and C to D. Next measure

across top of paper $3\frac{1}{8}''$ and then down $\frac{3}{4}''$ marking X for press stud position.

6. Trace back neck shape shown on draft pattern opposite by the double dash line in the same way as for front pattern; similarly trace back armhole.

Making tunic dress. Use pattern described above, which has turning allowances of $\frac{1}{4}''$ on neck and armhole, $\frac{1}{2}''$ on side seam and $1''$ for hem; $\frac{3}{4}$ yard of cotton or synthetic fabric and matching sewing thread.

1. To cut out the dress first press out material creases and fold lines, then fold in both selvedges to meet in the centre, making two folded edges on which to place the pattern pieces.

2. Place front pattern section on left fold and back on right fold, so that line A to B is exactly level with folded edge and hem is level with raw edge, pinning every $6''$ to $8''$.

3. Check that fabric pattern is right way up and then cut out accurately. Next cut neck and armhole facings all in one by repeating the fabric cut to a depth of $7''$, giving a double bodice. Alternatively cut separate crossway strips or buy bias binding.

4. Join side seams with simple flat fell method explained on page 113. Next join facing seams with an ordinary flat open seam.

5. Place front facing on to front of dress, right sides together,

and pin on shoulder, front and side, continuing for back facing. Stitch together $\frac{1}{4}''$ from edge all round neck, armholes and shoulder curves.

6. Turn facing to inside of dress and press flat. Next check length, then turn hem up and neaten. Finally neaten facing edges and stitch into position first by hand on the side seam junctions and then by top edge

something like those shown below—provided you follow the simple basic rules.

1. When considering the surface decoration, such as embroidery stitches, appliqué sections, novelty cut-outs or ready-made trimmings, first spend a little time experimenting before actually starting to stitch as quite often your first ideas can be improved on with a little

stitching $\frac{1}{8}''$ to $\frac{5}{8}''$ from folded edges as required, before adding a shoulder press stud or buttoned fastening.

Design adapting. If you have successfully made one beach tunic which fits reasonably well and would like to make another, you will find it very easy to adapt the same pattern to create a design of your own or

practice.

2. If you would like to add a pocket or a collar, try out various shapes in paper before cutting the material, using previously made collars and pockets as a guide. When the shape is correct, first mark the exact position on to the dress and then make the design detail in fabric, but remember to add

on a stitching turning allowance.
3. If you would like to add special edgings, insets or frills make sure that you know how to attach these correctly, by practising the simple methods explained on pages 50–53 and elsewhere in this book.
4. Keep a scrap-book of ideas, press photographs and how-to-do-it notes, so that whenever you feel in the mood

dress as explained on page 109. Next cut out several paper flower shapes and pin these into position, using dressmakers' chalk to indicate the embroidery stitches. If the various shapes look nice then unpin them one at a time, replacing them with coloured felt shapes cut to the exact size of the paper pieces. Stick them on with UHU glue before embroidering into

for making another dress you can refer to your book for ideas.
Making designs is fun. For instance, to make the simple flowered dress shown opposite you will need ¾ yard of plain fabric, several oddments of coloured felt, a selection of embroidery threads and two coloured buttons.

First cut out and make the

position. Finally add various extra stitches as explained on page 51, braiding as on page 92 and some beads as on page 54. Now try your skill at designing.
Beach rompers. To make the simple beach rompers shown overleaf you will require ½ yard of denim, medium weight cotton or similar fabric, two buttons, embroidery thread,

bias binding, sewing cotton and 1 yard of $\frac{1}{4}''$ elastic. To make the pattern you will need a sheet of plain wrapping paper, a sharp pencil and a ruler.

1. Working from the top left corner of the paper, A, measure down 12″ and mark dot B. Measure across top of paper 23″ and mark dot C. Now measure down from C 12″ and mark dot D—which should be 23″ from B. Draw straight lines to

mark other side from it, checking that both sharp curves are in the front and that each is 4″ deep, leaving 4″ between the middles.

3. Mark out a 6″ square for the front bib pattern, and a rectangle 16″ × 2″ for the shoulder straps. Cut all these pattern pieces out, and note the following turning allowances have been made: $\frac{1}{2}''$ side seam, $\frac{1}{4}''$ leg seam, 1″ waist turn-down, and a $\frac{1}{2}''$ on

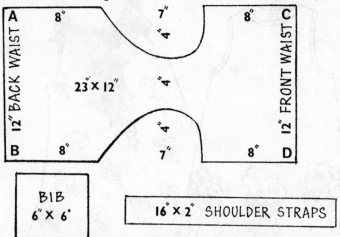

connect A, B, C and D.

2. Measure along line A to C and mark into three sections, 8″–7″–8″, drawing in the leg shape as shown in the diagram above. For accuracy first draw one elliptical shape 4″ deep, making a sharp curve for the front and a long gentler curve for the back. Trace this leg shape on to a piece of see-through greaseproof paper and

bib and shoulder straps.

Making rompers. Using the pattern described above, cut out the main section plus two bibs and four shoulder straps from $\frac{1}{2}$ yard of denim or cotton fabric.

1. Join the front and back 8″ side seams between A to C, and then B to D, with a simple flat fell seam, by placing the wrong sides of the fabric together and stitching through $\frac{1}{2}''$ from edge.

Trim the back turning down to ¼″ and then fold front turning over this, turning under ¼″ and stitching ⅛″ from fold through all thicknesses—as shown in diagram 1 on the right.

2. Face out leg area in bias binding by first stitching on the matching bias strip ¼″ from the edge and then turning both the strip and turning allowance through leg opening on to the wrong side and stitching, first ⅛″ from folded edge then ⅛″ from inside bias fold, right through all thicknesses. Slot 10″ of elastic between the bias facing and fabric, and draw up to leg size.

3. Make front bib by placing the two 6″ squares of fabric face to face and stitching around three sides ½″ in. Turn through so right sides are showing and press flat. Make shoulder straps similarly. Next crease over ¼″ all round top of rompers and fold, down ¾″, stitching first ⅛″ from fold and then ⅛″ from crease right through all fabric to form waistband. Place bib in centre of front so 1″ is below top fold, and secure with two stitched lines.

4. Slot in remaining 16″ of elastic through centre of waistband across back, attaching to each side of bib. Next sew on shoulder straps 1″ each side of centre back. Finally make two 1″ buttonholes 1″ from the top. Attach buttons and then add some decoration if required.

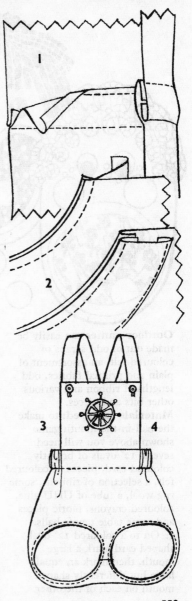

Outdoor games can easily be made out of odd scraps of coloured felt, an assortment of plain and printed fabrics, odd lengths of ribbon and various other bits and pieces.

Materials required: to make the ball-in-the-mouth game shown above you will need several 12″ ovals of brightly coloured card, pieces of coloured felt, a selection of ribbons, some rug wool, a tube of UHU glue, coloured crayons, fabric pieces and some table tennis balls.

1. On to a coloured 12″ oval shaped card mark a large mouth, then mark an equally large but differently shaped mouth on each of the other

cards. Cut out mouth and colour ½″ all round lip edge with coloured crayon.

2. Cut out two sixpenny-sized pieces of felt and then two half-crown-sized pieces of a contrasting colour. Stick smaller ones on to larger with UHU glue and then stick these into position for eyes. Cut two more large pieces for cheeks and stick into position if required.

3. Make hair with loops of rug wool and ribbon or fringed lengths of felt. Stick these, and felt ears if required, into position.

4. Stitch some coloured fabrics into a simple bag shape at least 2″ larger than the cardboard

mouth openings. Stick bag behind the mouth with the seam edges on the outside. Finally stick on a 12" cardboard back prop or suspend with string.

Make at least three of these with twelve coloured tennis balls for two children.

Racing animals. For this game you need to make several 4" to 6" animals of differing shapes and colours as explained on pages 12 and 13.

Materials required. Pieces of coloured felt, a ¾" brass curtain ring for each animal, several balls of string, pieces of ribbon, pieces of stocking for stuffing, oddments of wool, beads for eyes and some embroidery or sewing thread and various novelties etc.

1. Cut two identical animal shapes in coloured felt and stitch together ⅛" from edge but leaving 1½" open for stuffing. Fill until well padded with cut-up stocking pieces or other lightweight stuffing and then sew gap together.

2. Add felt ears, beaded eyes, rug wool hair, coloured feet, string tails and embroidered markings as required. Next sew on a ¾" brass ring across the back so that it stands upright and the hole is facing front and back.

3. In the same way make a variety of insects, fish and other animals. Cut string into 12 ft. lengths and tie one end to a stick or peg fixed to the ground, and pass the other end through the front of the ring. Fix other

animals into a line 12″ apart and then mark a finishing line 12″ in front of pegs.

The game is to jerk the string to move the animals forward, but not so strongly as to pull out the peg. To make the game more fun various obstacles can also be used.

Kite making. Materials required: three garden stakes 2 ft. 9″ long and just over ¼″ thick, 1 yard of thin but strong fabric, pieces of coloured felt, UHU glue, coloured tissue paper for the tail, a large ball of kite twine and a simple ¾″ metal ring.

1. Cut one stake to 2 ft. 6″ long and mark into equal 10″ sections. Mark 11″ from one end of each of the other two stakes. Lay the shorter stake on to the other two so that the 10″ marks cover the 11″ marks, forming an H shape, and bind firmly together with twine. Take the two long ends and place together and bind securely for 1″ as in top diagram.

2. Cut out ⅛″ deep notches at the end of each stick. Now stretch twine around the outside, preferably twice for safety, to form outer edge shape of kite.

3. Lay the kite frame on to the fabric and mark 1½″ larger all round before cutting out. Now lay frame on wrong side of fabric and fold seam allowances over the twine, pulling fairly taut and stitching turning into place.

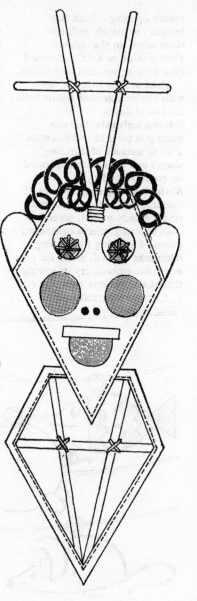

4. The next thing to do is decorate the front shape with cut-outs of brightly coloured felt pieces, sticking and stitching them into position as explained on page 94, adding other decorative ideas with the aid of coloured felt-tipped pens, etc. Also decorate 5 ft. length of twine with coloured bows of tissue paper and felt pieces to form a gay tail, then attach firmly to kite.

5. Cut two 2 ft. lengths of twine and attach one at each end of the 2 ft. 6″ crossway stick, and then attach a 2 ft. 9″ length to the tail end of kite. To attach these firmly, simply thread the twine through the fabric with a darning needle, ¾″ in from the edge and tightly against the side of the support sticks, then back tightly against the other side of the stick before knotting firmly. Bring all three loose ends together and knot on to a ¾″ metal curtain ring to form the flying guide strings.

6. Wind remaining kite twine round a fishing line winder, an old fishing reel or a 12″ length of thickish stick. Tie the free end on to the metal ring. Now try out the kite.

When flying it, first of all test to see if the flying guide strings and tail are hanging correctly. For instance, if the kite won't lift then the tail is probably too long and heavy. If it twists and spins then the

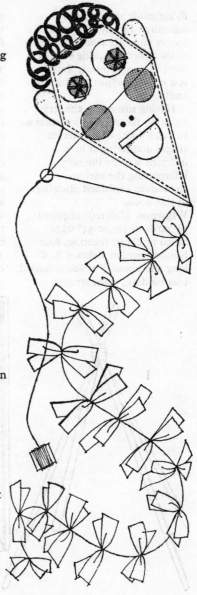

flying guide strings need adjusting. Finally, if the kite moves violently from one side to the other the guide strings need to be shortened. Simply test out and adjust until it flies really well.

Having made one kite, try adapting the making instructions to make a kite of a different shape, decorating it in a different way by liberally interpreting the various techniques explained elsewhere in this book.

Wigwam. Materials required: 3½ yards of 48″ or 54″ wide calico or cheap sheeting, four bamboo garden stakes 5 ft. 6″ long and about ¾″ thick, coloured bias binding, some strong

stitching cotton, 12″ of 1″ wide webbing or tape, several coloured felt-tip pens and some pieces of thin string.

1. First make the wigwam frame. Notch each stick 6″ from the top and then bind all four sticks together over the top of the notches. The notches will prevent the string from slipping when the frame stands as in diagram 1.

2. Cut the calico into two equal pieces, each 5 ft. 3″ long, and lay together so that selvedge edges meet. Stitch together ½″ from each edge and then fasten off securely.

3. Draw a straight line from the two bottom corners diagonally up the length to the middle of

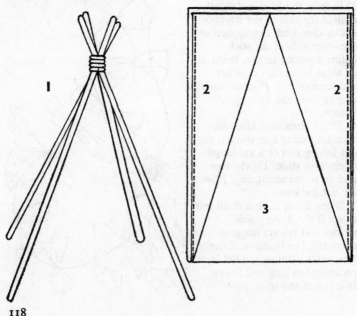

1

2   2

3

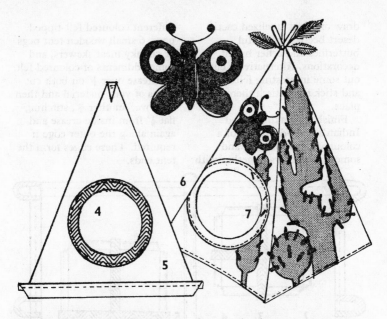

top edge, as shown in diagram
3, and then cut along these two
lines to give four triangular
sections: two with seams and
two without.

4. In the centre of one of the
unseamed sections mark a
circular or oval doorway big
enough for a child to crawl
through, using a large meat
plate or bucket lid as a guide
for shaping. Cut out this
section and bind the raw edges
with coloured bias binding.

5. On all four sections turn
down top point 3″ on to inside
and stitch ½″ from the fold
before trimming neatly. Along
hem first crease under ¼″ and
then fold on to wrong side
another 1″ before stitching ⅛″

from both edges.

6. Starting from the hem of
each triangular section and with
right sides facing each other,
stitch the right-hand diagonal
side of one piece to the
left-hand diagonal side of the
next, which is then seamed to
the third and so on until they
form a large cone shape. On to
the inside corner of each hem
edge sew on 3″ of 1″ webbing,
doubled over to form a little
bag into which the frame sticks
can be slotted.

7. Turn cone right sides out
and place over wigwam frame
to see how it fits, remembering
to slot bamboo ends into the
webbing bags.

Using the felt-tipped pens,

draw on giant stylized cacti, desert beetles, colourful butterflies and other bright decorations. Alternatively cut out some interesting felt shapes and stick then stitch them into place.

Finish by making a Red Indian's head-dress out of a coloured felt headband and some gay feathers, together with

different coloured felt-tipped pens, 6 small wooden tent pegs or chunky meat skewers, and some oddments of coloured felt.

1. Crease over ¼″ on both cut edges of your material and then fold over another ¾″, stitching flat ⅛″ from inside crease and again along the outer edge if required. These edges form the tent ends.

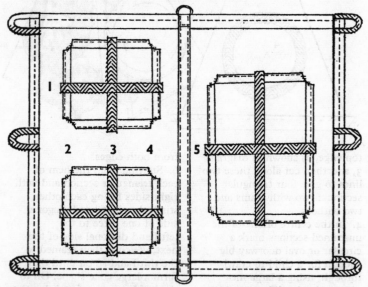

fringed trousers—as shown on page 57—and possibly a special hobby horse as explained on page 17.

Play tent. Materials required: 2½ yards of 48″ or 54″ wide calico or cheap unbleached sheeting, 6 yards of 1″ webbing or tape, two 1″ metal curtain rings, a ball of strong string, stitching thread, a selection of

Turn in both selvedge edges in the same way to form the ground edges.

2. Mark on window shapes as shown, two of which are 12″ × 12″, 20″ up from the hem and 8″ in from the sides, and the third 24″ × 12″, again 20″ up from the hem but 12″ in from each side.

3. Cut away the centre fabric

from each of the windows, leaving a 1" seam allowance around all edges. Snip into each corner and turn allowance on to wrong side and stitch flat, strengthening each snip with a few over stitches.

4. Cut webbing window bars 2" longer than the window opening and then stitch to the inside of each window at both ends and at each crossing. Cut

by figure 5 opposite. Leave an equal amount of webbing out at each end on to which the 1" metal curtain rings are slotted. Fold over the excess webbing and stitch flat to inside of tent.

6. Decorate outside of tent with giant brightly coloured flowers using a variety of felt-tipped pens, adding various felt cut-out shapes and other extras as required.

six 5" pieces of webbing and fold them in half to form loops for slotting in pegs. Stitch one on to each corner and another in the centre of each ground edge.

5. Cut a 5 ft. length of webbing and double edge stitch this into the centre of the tent along its entire length and exactly in between the windows, as shown

7. Tie a length of strong cord to each of the metal rings and then fasten the other ends to a post, tree or wall, before finally pegging the loops into the ground, adjusting the height and length of the strings as needed.

Finally make some firm play outfits as explained for fancy dress clothes on pages 56 to 59 together with a hobby horse as on page 17 and other toys etc.

A garden swing can soon be made to look very decorative by anybody who would like to try their hand at sewing the essential extras. The one illustrated on the left is basically an ordinary garden play swing which comes with all the necessary fixing points, side ropes and seat, though even these items could easily be made at home if you felt so inclined.

First fix the swing into a suitable position under a tree, on a patio or, if you prefer it, even inside a room. Make sure that the fixing loops are firm and the ropes properly secured.

Start by decorating the side ropes with pretty ribbons, colourful braids, dried flowers and other attractive things, adding several bows at the top and bottom of the side ropes.

Next cut a 2″ thick section of polythene foam or latex to fit on to the seat and form the basis of a cushion. Cut two rectangular sections of pretty printed cotton fabric, ½″ larger all round than the polythene shape, and then cut a gusset section 3″ wide—i.e., 1″ wider than the foam shape—to go right round, plus extra for side seams.

Joint all these sections together as for an ordinary cushion—explained on pages 78 and 79—but remembering to leave one side open for slotting in the foam shape.

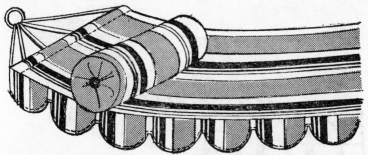

Attach this cushion to the swing with ribbons and bows, etc.

Garden hammock. Materials required: 2½ yards of strong striped deckchair canvas, 7 yards of carpet webbing for binding, 10 yards of strong upholstery webbing for end hanging supports, two 2″–3″ solid metal rings from an ironmongers, a box of upholstery nails, two 1″ thick hardwood dowels the same width as the deckchair canvas, a heavy duty machining needle—15 × 1 size 18 or 19 for most makes—and some strong matching thread, a carpet needle and line carpet thread.

1. Bind the two long sides of the deckchair canvas with the carpet webbing, using a strong machine thread and heavy duty needle. To bind accurately first cut a 2½ yard length of webbing and press the width in half right along this length, making sure that the edges meet exactly all the way along. Slot the deckchair canvas in between this fold, first tacking and then machining right through ¼″ from inside edge.

2. Turn over 2½″ at each end of canvas to form the dowel casing and then machine stitch ½″ from the raw edge right through both thicknesses in between the webbing, but preferably hand-stitching both sides to avoid breaking the

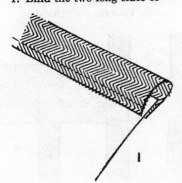

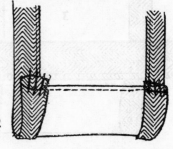

1   2

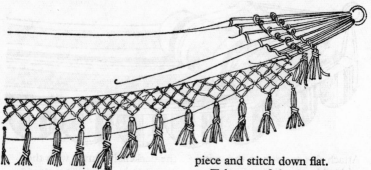

machine needle. You will find that a carpet needle and linen thread stab-stitched and then overcast is strongest.

3. Stitch on a piece of carpet webbing so that it butts against the two turned-in raw edges on each end, but leave 2″ protruding each side as in diagram 3 above. Turn in this 2″ allowance at each end and then turn webbing over to cover stitches, thus forming a flange.

4. Insert the 1″ thick hardwood dowel into end casing. Now cut the upholstery webbing into four equal sections 2½ yards long. Turn in 1″ at both ends of each

piece and stitch down flat.

5. Take one of the prepared upholstery webbing strips and tuck one end under the carpet webbing flange 1″ in from the edge. Using four strong upholstery nails, nail through the flange, upholstery webbing, the canvas and into the centre of the dowel. Similarly attach the three remaining pieces of upholstery webbing to the other corners, using four nails for each piece.

6. Next take the left-hand webbing strip and slot it through the special 3″ solid metal ring, then nail it into position 2″ beyond the exact centre. Take the right-hand

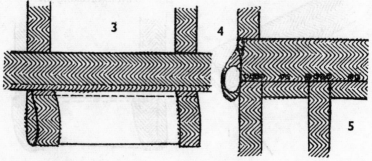

webbing and slot it through the metal ring, nailing it 2″ beyond the other side of centre so that the webbing strips cross each other but lay flat as they pass through the loop. Nail the various gaps flat every 3″ between each strap.

7. Make two bolster cushions from an extra length of matching or contrasting fabric, using the instructions set out on pages 78 and 99, before finally looping the strong suspension ropes through each end ring and securing safely between two suitable trees or other firm fixings.

Edgings. The easiest of all edgings to attach is the simple string fringe, which can either be bought by the yard or made.

1. Make a simple crochet looped chain, as shown above, and then pin this to the side of a cardboard box so that the loops are facing downwards.

2. Cut some 8″ to 10″ lengths of string by winding the string around a 4″ or 5″ strip of firm cardboard and then cutting along one of the folds.

Slot six of the folded edges through each loop and then slot the strand ends through the fold before pulling tight.

3. If you would like a knotted fringe, as shown below right, then the strand lengths should be cut 12″ to 18″ deep by winding them around a 6″ or 9″ strip of firm cardboard, then slotting through in the same

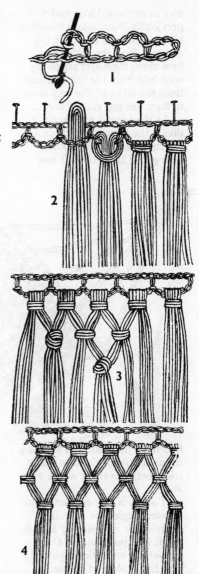

125

way as explained in 1 and 2 previously. Next take a bunch of hanging threads from the left and half from the right, and knot them together; repeating with half from the left and half from the right all the way along to form the top row of knots.
4. In the second row, again divide the bunches of threads which hang from each knot, taking half from the left and

could also be used, such as scallops, dagging or tasselled edges, bobble fringing, cotton crochet, embroidered strips, appliquéd and bound sections, looped tassels, felt stick-ons, or indeed any of the surface decorations mentioned in this or our other 'Streamlined Sewing' books. Simply look around for

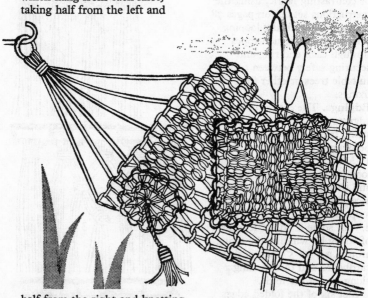

half from the right and knotting together so that the new knots come between those of the row above.
5. To attach this crocheted and knotted edging, or a similar ready-made one, simply surface-pin it into position and then stab-stitch on to the edge with matching coloured cotton.

Other decorative edgings

new ideas and choose the one you would particularly like for your own garden hammock.
Other ideas. Apart from those mentioned in this chapter, you could of course apply any of your own ideas when sewing for out-of-doors; ideas that incorporate unusual colourings, exciting textures and bold

designs and which do not have to be limited to compromise with any indoor decoration. The previous twenty-nine pages will have given you an introduction to sewing for out-of-doors, the general methods of sewing being intended to be liberally interpreted to help you develop original ideas of your own.

magazines and newspapers, as well as noticing things in friends' houses and on TV to get ideas. Collect together as many notes, press cuttings, pictures and samples of materials as possible, so that whenever you are in the mood to create something new you will only have to refer to your scrap-book

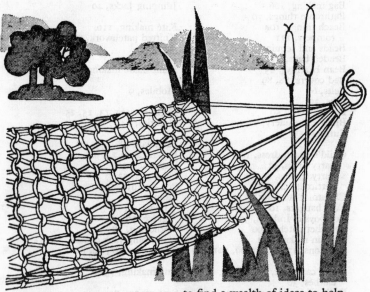

Remember that the most rewarding aspect of any needlework is seeing a finished article which is entirely your own creation, and which, into the bargain, you have thoroughly enjoyed making. It is well worth spending a little time browsing through shops and stores, thumbing through

to find a wealth of ideas to help crystallize your thoughts, in much the same way as using a cookery book.

Finally, if you think of your needlework as a creative art which has no inhibiting rules, you will find that your sewing is not only quick and easy to do, but also thoroughly enjoyable and fun as well.

Index